What Christian Leaders are saying about *Born to Grow*

◆———◆)(◆———◆

"*Born to Grow* by Pierre Eade provides any Christian seeking to personally worship God in spirit and truth with a wonderful, practical guide for spiritual maturing in Christ. This thoughtful book provides profound biblical, historical, and pragmatic instruction for drawing closer to God through spiritual discipline. Journey through its pages and be abundantly blessed."

– Robert Sterns, Founder and Executive Director of Eagles' Wings

"So many Christian books make Christian growth into a chore— almost a legalistic, prescriptive, nearly impossible task. You must read Pierre Eade's *Born to Grow*. His delightful humor, stories, insights, and growing tips will encourage, motivate, and empower you in the joyful journey of spiritual growth in Christ. Take the journey. This book will take you somewhere Good with God!"

– Dr. Larry Keefauver, Bestselling Christian Author, International Teacher

"Take the journey of spiritual growth from one of the Church's most promising young authors. *Born to Grow* is refreshing, insightful and inspiring! It is one of the most enjoyable books that I have read in a long time. Take it from me, if you want to grow in your walk with God, read this book."

– Dr. Scott Mcdermott, Lead Pastor, New Testament Scholar, International Speaker

"Pierre Eade has a flare for writing that tickles the mind. Furthermore the sensitive encouragement to grow in faith with humility, courage, and grace are inspiring and hopeful. I highly recommend *Born to Grow* to nurture and spur you on in Christ."

– Dr. Scott Turansky, Author of *Parenting is Heart Work*

"Through a fun and witty exploration of the Christian life, Pierre Eade presents four ways every Christian must grow to really enjoy intimacy with Abba Father. You'll love the stories and practical teaching Pierre presents as you take the journey to the good place God has for your life."

– Michael J. Pfau, M.Ed., Professional Life Coach, Speaker and Author

"With compelling stories, gentle humor, and practical steps, *Born to Grow* is an indispensible companion on your journey closer to God. This book will both inspire and equip you to experience the fullness of who you were designed to be."

Kim Avery, MA, Professional Counselor, Board Certified Life Coach, Author and Speaker

Margie,
you were...
Born to Grow!
Pierre
2 Peter 3:18

BORN TO GROW

You're Growing Somewhere Good!

Pierre M. Eade

www.xulonpress.com

In Loving Memory of Edward Elias Eade

Thank you for living such a vibrant life for Jesus Christ. It's all good!

Dedication

Mom and Dad, I dedicate this book to you. Thank you for doing such an amazing job raising our family. I don't quite know how you managed it all, but I will be forever grateful for the upbringing you gave me.

Table of Contents

Acknowledgments

Irst and foremost, I need to acknowledge God my Father for loving me enough to send Jesus to save me. I didn't deserve it, but am truly grateful for your undying love, Jesus. Thank you, Holy Spirit for the inspiration!

I owe special thanks to several people who came across my path and influenced my writing. First, a thanks goes out to Rob Marshall and his wife Sherry who took a risk to allow a stranger and potential serial killer to stay in their home. My time at your church was instrumental in bringing about this book. Thank you, Donald Newman from Xulon Press, for encouraging me to write from my life passion. Thank you, Jeff Stormer, for your coaching and encouragement to keep writing fervently and not give up. Thank you, Matt Deeter for your generosity of heart and helping make a dream become a reality. Thank you, Dr. Larry Keefauver, for your editorial excellence and encouraging words along the path.

Thank you Pastor Alan Oliver for sharing the gospel with me on that memorable plane ride from Paris, France in November of 1998. My life has not been the same ever since. Thank you, Michael Goetz for the time spent with me as a young Christian man, breakfast after breakfast, year after year. I wouldn't be where I am today without you. May God continue to give you great returns on your investments!

I want to thank my brothers and sisters for helping the baby of the family grow up. You have each contributed to my life in a special way. Eddie, thank you for showing me how not to live and how to live all in one lifetime. I still miss you. Thank you brother Paul for modeling to me what it means to be strong, but gentle and showing me such great brotherly love. Thank you, Paula, for being such a model of hard work and love in action. Thank you, Michele for teaching me what it means to make a plan and "Execute the plan." Mary, thank you for my first Bible. Now look at me! Who would have thought?

Amanda, thank you for being my companion, friend, confidant and beautiful wife. Thank you for doing God's work at home so I can do God's work out in the world. I love you. Elijah, Jordan and Olivia, you inspire me every day to love God more and become a better man. May you grow beyond me! I love you.

Introduction

Digging for Hidden Treasure

As a kid I always enjoyed searching for the toy at the bottom of the cereal box. I would tip the box to one side trying to dig a hole deep enough to discover the hidden treasure. If that didn't work, I'd trying sticking my grubby little fingers deep down inside the box to search for the plastic sealed bag. (I apologize to my brothers and sisters who had no idea that my hands had been in their cereal!) And if my hands couldn't reach, I'd call in Mom to the rescue. She would pour the whole bag of cereal into a bowl just so I could get the five cent toy hidden in my Cap'n Crunch®. Why on earth did they bury those toys so deep?

Imagine your life is like a box of cereal. You may be something healthy, like Kashi® or something fruity like Fruit Loops®. You may be sweet, filled with sugar or dry and packed with fiber. You may be an oversized family box or a little mini sample sized box. Whatever your size, shape, box design or level of sweetness, there is a hidden treasure within you. Unlike the five cent toy that I was so desperate to find, this treasure is something so precious and valuable that God has given His all to bring it out.

Shortly after I became a Christian in my early twenties, God showed me four distinct treasures that He was seeking to grow in the lives of His children. The treasures God is developing within you have more to do with what's inside your box than how your box looks on the outside. The treasures have been purchased by God in advance and are now just waiting to be discovered as you search them out.

My goal in this book is three-fold. First, I hope to **inspire you** to dig deep for God's treasure. The marketing department of those cereal companies understood how to tantalize little girls and boys like me to want that toy bad enough to dig deep. My hope is that through the words I've penned you too will be inspired to grow in your relationship with God like never before.

Secondly, my goal is to **teach you.** Getting the treasure out of a cereal box takes a certain amount of knowledge as much as it does skill. First, you need to know the treasure exists. Then you need to know the approximate location of the treasure. Lastly, you need to learn the tips and tricks of finding the treasure and digging it out. In the pages ahead you will learn new facts and be reminded of great truths that will help you on your spiritual treasure quest.

Finally, my goal is to **lead and empower you.** From one treasure seeker to another, I am going to speak to you from my own heart and experience in order to help you follow not in my own footsteps, but in the greater footsteps of God the Father, Son and Holy Spirit. I am on this journey with you and while I have the privilege of leading the trip, my hope is that you will also take off from my lead and discover new paths of your own. If my words lead you to run faster or ahead of me, I've done my job.

So what is this wonderful treasure we are seeking to find? It is the treasure of God's life being nurtured within you so that you may grow into the type of person He has destined you to be. "For God [wants you] to know that the riches and glory of Christ are for you...too. And this is the secret: Christ lives in you. This gives you assurance of sharing his glory" (Colossians 1:27, NLT).

May the words you are about to read inspire, teach, lead and empower you to grow into the person God has designed you to become even before the day you were born. You were born to grow!

How to Make the Most of this Book

One of my favorite words in the French language is the verb *prof-iter* (pro-fee-tay). Similar to the idea of profiting, this verb means to make the most out of a particular situation. So say for example, it's a beautiful day outside and a great day for some exercise or a walk outdoors. I could encourage you to go for it by simply saying, "Profitez!" Make the most of it. Get it for what it's worth.

My hope is that you will really "profiter" from this book in a major way. And in order to help you be profitable in your reading I want to give you several tips and tools.

1. **Read the book** – Let's start with the basics. A book on the shelf is no comparison to a book in one's hands. I have many books on my shelves at home and inside my Kindle app that have never been completely read. I have treasure still left to be discovered! Don't leave any treasure behind, read this book to the end.

2. **Remember These Truths & Take Action** – At the end of each chapter I have summarized some of the key points under this caption. Repetition is one of the greatest teachers we have in life. Read over these truths and then make a determination to take some action based on what you have learned and how God is leading you.

3. **Personal Reflection and Group Discussion Questions** – The more work you put in on your end the more you will get out of this book. Take some time at the end of each chapter by yourself and God or with some friends to discuss what you read and to answer some or all of the questions in this section. Your conversation and thoughts will take you further than my own words alone.

4. **Meditation** – I have tried to distill each chapter down into one simple sentence of truth that is easy to repeat over and

over in your mind. If you take a few moments to get still, quiet and focused on this one sentence it can have the power to further nurture the truth within you. Repeat it in your head, then say it out loud and tell it to yourself again and again.

5. **Prayer** – I have included a simple one line prayer at the end of every chapter. Some chapters end with a longer prayer as well, but all of them have this one liner for you to pray. I decided not to make this a complicated prayer, but an easy one to repeat or even memorize. Prayer is our life line to God and for this reason will add even greater power to your book reading.

6. **Bible References** – At the end of every chapter I have noted all the Bible references that were used within the chapter. You can take this information and look up the Scriptures in your preferred Bible translation. You may want to memorize one of those verses, do a further study of the verse in context or post the verse on-line to share with friends.

7. **Share with others** – The benefits of this book are not meant to be kept to yourself. Find a few friends to read this book together with you and share your experiences. Recommend this book to a friend or buy a copy as a gift to someone you think would find it beneficial.

Profitez!

Chapter 1

A Life of Continual Growth

"Tony's pitching." The two most dreaded words every little leaguer feared hearing. It would make my stomach turn like the words "Pop Quiz." "Tony's pitching." "Tony's pitching." "Tony's pitching." In 1985, Tony Capito was the fastest pitcher in all Little League back in our small hometown of Olean, New York. As the ball flew from Tony's hand it would make a sound similar to the candy whistles we would buy at the concession stand after the game. The leather ball would strike the catcher's leather glove and make a thunderous clap like a whip against a horse's hide.

No batter in his right mind liked facing Tony Capito on the mound. When you heard the news, "Tony's pitching" before the start of the game, you began to wonder if it was too late to call in sick. Facing Tony as a batter was not only intimidating, it was downright scary. One wild pitch could mean decapitation. If I were to be ever so lucky to make contact with the ball (an unlikely event), my hands would sting for a good couple minutes. Fear. Pain. Intimidation. I should have been a wrestler.

What made Tony so intimidating was not just his fastball. It was his size. Tony had already outgrown his Dad and coach in height—which did not take much since his Dad was all of five foot six inches at best. Tony's appearance added to the intimidation. By the time the game was over, Tony had a five o'clock shadow. Tony was big, hairy, and most of all tough. Maybe a more accurate word was mean!

Tony's intimidation factor diminished over the years. (I still could not hit his fastball, but that had more to do with my lame swing than anything else.) His intimidation diminished because he stopped growing. The beastly looking Tony Capito at age nine was the same size Tony at age nineteen. He never grew another inch! Well, actually, that is not true. I think he did grow a bit tougher over time. He was still quite an after school brawler for his size. I am sure his facial hair development continued to blossom with age. As for height, however, Tony was done growing. The growth spurt he had in elementary school never carried over into junior high or high school. He went from being off the charts to hardly on them.

We can all relate to Tony, not necessarily because we were the tallest kids in our fifth grade class or had full facial hair before we were old enough to drive. We can relate to Tony because all of us at some point in our life stopped growing. Your growth spurts may have ended in elementary school or you may have been one of those late bloomers who did not start growing until you were out of high school. In any case, at some point or another, you stopped getting taller.

God has a tremendous plan for each of our lives. His plan is for us to **grow** continually. Not the type of growth that will get you drafted into the NBA or allow you to pick bananas without needing to learn how to climb trees. The type of growth that God has in mind for you is beyond your genetic predisposition. God has a plan for you to grow in four distinct ways.

Grow Up, Grow Out, Grow Deeper, and Grow Together

God plans for you to "Grow Up" meaning He wants you to become more mature in your thinking, attitude, and behavior. He has a plan for you to "Grow Out" which is how He wants to use your life to positively impact other people in this world. He has a plan for you to "Grow Deeper" in relationship with Him. He has a plan for you to "Grow Together" with other people who are likeminded and on this same pathway to growth. Grow Up. Grow Out. Grow Deeper. Grow Together. That is God's plan for you.

Imagine with me for a moment if Tony Capito never stopped growing. I mean never. Today, Tony would be about 23 feet tall (trust me I did the math), and weigh somewhere around 527 pounds. Let us not even talk about the hair! Giraffes would look up to him. Lions would crown him king. Every professional sports team would look to draft him. He would be a modern day giant. Goliath would need his own slingshot to take this guy down!

Now I know what you are thinking, "Real funny, but let's get real. No human can grow to that size." Immediately, we start to limit the idea by our preconceived understanding of human growth patterns and reality. Truthfully many of us have greater spiritual growth potential than we could ever imagine. Yet we stop short of God's plan because we do not consider it possible. We consider what it would take to get there and we drop the idea like a New Year's Resolution in February.

Yet, God's ultimate goal for you to is to **grow**! Do you want to know specifically what God's growth goal is for you? It is actually the same goal He has for every man, woman, and child on the planet. How God does it is unique, but the end goal is the same. God's growth plan for you can be summarized in one sentence found in the Bible.

For those God foreknew he also predestined to be conformed to the image of his Son, that he might be the firstborn among many brothers and sisters. (Romans 8:29 NIV)

I want to break the meaning of this verse down for you, but not without first taking a commercial break from our sponsors. "Wheaties® is the breakfast of champions!"[1] End of break. Now back to the show. Seriously, have you ever considered the people you meet on a Wheaties® box? No average athlete makes it to the front cover of the "breakfast of champions." You have to be one of the best. Just think through the

---

[1] Wheaties® has in no way sponsored this book. And they also have not yet figured out that I would look amazingly cool on the front of their cereal boxes. If you are on the Wheaties® marketing team, you can reach me via my website to start discussing a contract: www.christiangrowthnetwork.com. I look forward to hearing from you.

names for a moment: Lou Gehrig, Mary Lou Retton, Walter Payton, Arnold Palmer, Dale Earnhardt, Muhammed Ali, Michael Jordan, and the infamous Little Leaguer pitcher, Tony Capito. Okay, Tony never made the cover of a Wheaties® box, but he is still a champion in my book.

Now imagine with me for a moment that God came down in a cloud and said, "I want to make you the next Michael Jordan."

After I got done laughing, I would go back to eating my Wheaties.® Then perhaps the conversation might go something like this:

"I want to make you the next Michael Jordan!"

"Sounds like a plan God, but I would be happy with just being able to hit a Tony Capito fastball if you would not mind."

"No! I have planned before the foundation of the earth that you will be just like Michael Jordan."

Okay, three times is enough. God is serious on this one.

"I will be the next Michael Jordan. I will be the next Michael Jordan. I will be the next Michael Jordan."

Now as outrageous and good as being the next Michael Jordan sounds (especially to a guy like me who loves basketball), it is nowhere close to reaching God's intentions and plan for my life or yours. Not even close! Becoming the next Michael Jordan would fall desperately short of God's plan for your life because God's plan is for you to become a perfect representation of His Son, Jesus Christ. He wants you to live like Him, to think like Him, to behave like Him, and to be so aligned with the personality and character of Jesus that when people meet you they feel like they have encountered and met Jesus.

That is what Romans 8:29 means when it says that before time God planned for us to be "conformed to the image of his Son." He planned before the foundation of the world that you and I would become more like Jesus. To become like Jesus Christ is more beautiful and larger than the neck of a giraffe, more amazing than a high flying dunk of Jordan, and at the same time more daunting than the fastball of Tony Capito.

This Is Why We All Need to Grow!

We need to "Grow Up" in Christ by developing greater spiritual maturity. Jesus never displayed an ounce of immaturity in all His time on earth. I know for some of you that sounds a bit boring, but boring and mature are not synonymous. Watching golf on TV and boring are synonymous, but mature and boring are not. Jesus was the life of every party He went to; and trust me, He went to His fair share. He was the talk of the town, and the most intriguing human of all ages. Still to this day, over 2000 years since His birth, He has more followers on earth than you have on both Twitter and Facebook combined times one-hundred. Yet Jesus was never immature. That is God's plan for you as well, to grow into a fully mature representation of the person of Jesus Christ.

We need to "Grow Out" in order to become more like Jesus Christ. Jesus was not afraid to mix with people of different races, social backgrounds, financial portfolios, religions, ages, and gender. In fact, this got Him in quite a bit of trouble with His onlookers and religious critics. "The Son of Man came eating and drinking, and you say, 'Here is a glutton and a drunkard, a friend of tax collectors and sinners'" (Luke 7:34). Jesus, the incarnation of life itself, brought life to every party He attended.

Many who claim to be followers of Christ today would never dare set foot in a party scene similar to where Jesus went in His day. It would be too unholy for us. Yet Jesus, the fully mature one (which translated can also be said as the Completely Holy One) was not afraid to mix with crowds of people who were not like the religious people of His day. God is calling you to do the same. God is calling you to "Grow Out" in your ability to reach people who are the outsiders, the down and outers, and the up and comers. The people who may have some interest in Jesus, but never frequent a church except for major holidays, weddings, and funerals are also on your target list. You cannot do that at church, you must "Grow Out."

All this growing up and out will require you to "Grow Deeper." You find a peculiar pattern in Jesus' life. One minute He is the center of attention with crowds of people hovering over Him, and the next minute He is by Himself in nature, that is until the crowds found out where He went! Jesus was one moment like a rock star on stage and the next moment like a monk in hiding.

Where did He go? He went to find a quiet place where He could spend time with God whom He called, "Daddy." Jesus had the most unique, intimate, and real relationship with God. Speaking of himself Jesus said, "The Son can do nothing by himself; he can do only what he sees his Father doing, because whatever the Father does the Son also does" (John 5:19b). Jesus was fully in synch with God.

God's desire for your life is that you would "Grow Deeper" in your relationship with Him so you too can be in synch, connected, and plugged into what He has for your life—a deep loving relationship.

Last and certainly not least, God wants you to "Grow Together" with other people. You would think that a man like Jesus would operate along the same lines as other superheroes we admire. He would be a man of isolation with a sense of mystery around Him because no one gets to know the "real Jesus" too well. He would be a lone ranger of sorts. The fact of the matter is that Jesus was anything but a soloist. He deliberately chose a dozen guys to do life with Him. He was not only intentional about hand selecting His own posse; He was intentional about spending time with them doing everything from the mundane to the supernatural. Jesus was building more than just an organization, He made those around Him feel like family sometimes to the exclusion of His own blood relatives (Matthew 12:46-50).

If we are going to be like Jesus as God wants us to be, we will need to take off some of our masks and open ourselves to the emotionally vulnerable world of real heart to heart relationships. Yes, we will need to "Grow Together."

Friend, the plan God has for your life is bigger, better, deeper, wider, taller, and more wonderful than you can ever think or even dream. His plan is to mold and model you into a person who actually lives like Jesus! As you can imagine, that is going to take a lot of growth!

God has also provided everything necessary for you to get from where you are to where He wants you to grow in life. I am not saying it will be easy. In fact, at times you will get those same butterflies in your stomach that I had when I heard, "Tony is pitching." But do not be discouraged and do not fake sick. I can promise you this—no wait, God can promise you this, it will be good for you in every way.

Are you ready? Let's grow!

Remember These Truths & Take Action

- God's plan is for you to **grow** continually.
- God's ultimate goal is for you to become like Jesus Christ.
- God plans for you to grow in four distinct ways:
    ○ Grow up (Maturity)
    ○ Grow out (Outreach)
    ○ Grow deeper (Loving God)
    ○ Grow together (Loving Others)

Personal Reflection and Group Discussion Questions

- What attitude or mindset would you need to have in order to grow continually?
- God's plan is for you to be *"conformed to the image of his Son" (Romans 8:29 NIV). What does being conformed to the image of Jesus look like?*
- *Which of the four areas of growth (up, out, deeper, together) do you feel you currently need the most work on?*

Meditation

God wants me to grow continually.

Prayer

God, help me to never stop growing up, growing out,
growing deeper or growing together.

Bible References

- Romans 8:29
- Luke 7:34
- John 5:19
- Matthew 12:46-50

 # WAYS TO PRAY
for an Unbeliever

Pierre M. Eade

1. Pray for Jesus to save them from their sins.

"She will give birth to a son, and you are to give him the name Jesus, because he will save his people from their sins." (Matthew 1:21, NIV)

2. Pray for the soil of their heart to receive the seeds of God's Word.

"Still other seed fell on good soil. It came up, grew and produced a crop, some multiplying thirty, some sixty, some a hundred times." (Mark 4:8, NIV)

3. Pray they will come home to the Father and receive his love and compassion.

"So he got up and went to his father. But while he was still a long way off, his father saw him and was filled with compassion for him; he ran to his son, threw his arms around him and kissed him." (Luke 15:20, NIV)

4. Pray for them to experience God's love firsthand.

"For God so loved the world, that he gave his only Son, that whoever believes in him should not perish but have eternal life." (John 3:16, ESV)

5. Pray they will hear the shepherd's voice and choose to follow him.

"I have other sheep that are not of this sheep pen. I must bring them also. They too will listen to my voice, and there shall be one flock and one Shepherd." (John 10:16, NIV)

6. Pray for God to open their eyes and turn them from darkness to light.

"To open their eyes and turn them from darkness to light, and from the power of Satan to God, so that they may receive forgiveness of sins and a place among those who are sanctified by faith in me." (Acts 26:18, NIV)

7. Pray for the power of God to bring them to salvation.

"For I am not ashamed of the gospel, because it is the power of God that brings salvation to everyone who believes: first to the Jew, then to the Gentile." (Romans 1:16, NIV)

8. Pray that God's kindness will lead them to repentance.

"Or do you show contempt for the riches of his kindness, forbearance and patience, not realizing that God's kindness is intended to lead you to repentance?" (Romans 2:4, NIV)

9. Pray for them to recognize their sin and need of a Savior.

"For all have sinned and fall short of the glory of God." (Romans 3:23, NIV)

10. Pray for them to be delivered from the wages of their sin.

"For the wages of sin is death, but the free gift of God is eternal life through Christ Jesus our Lord." (Romans 6:23, NLT)

11. Pray for the message of the cross to be revealed to their heart.

"For the word of the cross is foolishness to those who are perishing, but to us who are being saved it is the power of God." (1 Corinthians 1:18, NASB)

12. Pray for the light of God to shine in their heart.

"For God, who said, "Let light shine out of darkness," made his light shine in our hearts to give us the light of the knowledge of God's glory displayed in the face of Christ." (2 Corinthians 4:6, NIV)

13. Pray for God to rescue them from this evil world.

"Jesus gave his life for our sins, just as God our Father planned, in order to rescue us from this evil world in which we live." (Galatians 1:4, NLT)

14. Pray for them to receive God's gift of salvation by grace through faith.

"For by grace you have been saved through faith. And this is not your own doing; it is the gift of God." (Ephesians 2:8, ESV)

15. Pray they encounter Christians who shine brightly.

"So that you may be blameless and pure, children of God who are faultless in a crooked and perverted generation, among whom you shine like stars in the world." (Philippians 2:15, HCSB)

16. **Pray for God to deliver them from the domain of darkness into the kingdom of love.**

    "He has delivered us from the domain of darkness and transferred us to the kingdom of his beloved Son." (Colossians 1:13, ESV)

17. **Pray for the gospel to come to them not only in word, but in the power of the Holy Spirit.**

    "For our gospel came not unto you in word only, but also in power, and in the Holy Ghost, and in much assurance; as ye know what manner of men we were among you for your sake." (1 Thessalonians 1:5, KJV)

18. **Pray for the Lord to lead their heart into a full understanding and expression of God's love.**

    "May the Lord lead your hearts into a full understanding and expression of the love of God and the patient endurance that comes from Christ." (2 Thessalonians 3:5, NLT)

19. **Pray for Christ Jesus to save them from the depth of their sins.**

    "Here is a trustworthy saying that deserves full acceptance: Christ Jesus came into the world to save sinners--of whom I am the worst." (1 Timothy 1:15, NIV)

20. **Pray for God to change their heart so they can learn and receive the truth.**

    "Gently instruct those who oppose the truth. Perhaps God will change those people's hearts, and they will learn the truth." (2 Timothy 2:25, NLT)

21. **Pray for God to show them mercy that they may be regenerated and renewed.**

    "He saved us - not by works of righteousness that we had done, but according to His mercy -- through the washing of regeneration and renewal by the Holy Spirit." (Titus 3:5, HCSB)

22. **Pray for the grace of the Lord Jesus Christ to come upon their spiritual life.**

    "The grace of the Lord Jesus Christ be with your spirit." (Philemon 1:25, ESV)

23. **Pray they will not ignore such a great gift of salvation.**

    "How shall we escape if we ignore so great a salvation? This salvation, which was first announced by the Lord, was confirmed to us by those who heard him." (Hebrews 2:3, NIV)

24. **Pray for them to be converted, saved from death and from a multitude of sins.**

    "Let him know, that he which converteth the sinner from the error of his way shall save a soul from death, and shall hide a multitude of sins." (James 5:20, KJV)

25. **Pray for God to protect them by His power and give them the gift of salvation.**

    "You are being protected by God's power through faith for a salvation that is ready to be revealed in the last time." (1 Peter 1:5, HCSB)

26. **Pray for the Lord to show them patience and bring them to repentance.**

    "The Lord is not slow in keeping his promise, as some understand slowness. Instead he is patient with you, not wanting anyone to perish, but everyone to come to repentance." (2 Peter 3:9, NIV)

27. **Pray for them to confess their sins that they may be cleansed from all unrighteousness.**

    "If we confess our sins, He is faithful and righteous to forgive us our sins and to cleanse us from all unrighteousness." (1 John 1:9, NASB)

28. **Pray for God to show them grace, mercy and peace.**

    "Grace, mercy and peace from God the Father and from Jesus Christ, the Father's Son, will be with us in truth and love." (2 John 1:3, NIV)

29. **Pray for them to prosper and be blessed in body, mind and spirit.**

    "Dear friend, I pray that you may prosper in every way and be in good health physically just as you are spiritually." (3 John 1:2, HCSB)

30. **Pray for God to be glorified in and through their life.**

    "To the only wise God our Savior, be glory and majesty, dominion and power, both now and ever. Amen." (Jude 1:25, KJV)

31. **Pray for them to hear Christ knocking at the door of their heart to let Him in!**

    "Here I am! I stand at the door and knock. If anyone hears my voice and opens the door, I will come in and eat with that person, and they with me." (Revelation 3:20, NIV)

I am **ONE** with God.
"But whoever is united with the Lord is **ONE** with Him in spirit." (1 Corinthians 6:17, NIV))

I am **PROTECTED** by God.
"And through your faith, God is **PROTECTING** you by His power until you receive this salvation, which is ready to be revealed on the last day for all to see." (1 Peter 1:5, NLT)

I am **QUIET**.
"Make it your goal to live a **QUIET** life, minding your own business and working with your hands, just as we instructed you before." (1 Thessalonians 4:11, NLT)

I am **RELYING** on God's love.
"And so we know and **RELY** on the love God has for us. God is love. Whoever lives in love lives in God, and God in them." (1 John 4:16, NIV)

I am **STRONG** in the Lord.
"Finally, be **STRONG** in the Lord and in His mighty power." (Ephesians 6:10, BSB)

I am **TRUSTING** God.
"In God I have put my **TRUST**, I shall not be afraid. What can man do to me?" (Psalm 56:11, NASB)

I am **UNDERSTOOD** by God.
"This High Priest of ours **UNDERSTANDS** our weaknesses, for He faced all of the same testings we do, yet He did not sin." (Hebrews 4:15, NLT)

I am **VICTORIOUS**.
"Dear children, you belong to God. So you have won the **VICTORY** over these people, because the one who is in you is greater than the one who is in the world." (1 John 4:4, GW)

I am **WALKING** by faith.
"For we **WALK** by faith, not by sight." (2 Corinthians 5:7, KJV)

I am **EXCEEDINGLY** blessed.
"Now to Him that is able to do **EXCEEDING** abundantly above all that we ask or think, according to the power that works in us." (Ephesians 3:20, AKJV)

I am **YOUNG, but Godly.**
"Don't let anyone look down on you because you are **YOUNG**, but set an example for the believers in speech, in conduct, in love, in faith and in purity." (1 Timothy 4:12, NIV)

I am **ZEALOUS**.
"Never be lacking in **ZEAL**, but keep your spiritual fervor, serving the Lord." (Romans 12:11, NIV)

The Importance of Knowing Your Identity in Christ

The ABCs of Your Identity in Christ was first created to teach children how God sees them. Children are being exposed to a broad range of messages from TV, the Internet, School, Friends, Neighbors and Social Media. The messages they receive are not neutral. Our kids are being taught intentionally and subliminally who they are and what makes them important or not. If we do not step in as a parent, guardian or spiritual leader to teach our children their identity in Christ, our kids will determine their value and worth based on the messages of our culture. Now that's a scary thought! For this reason, it is vitally important to teach our kids who they are in Christ.

Although The ABCs of Your Identity in Christ were initially created for kids, they are just as helpful and powerful for adults. As believers in Jesus, we need to find our true identity, security and rest in our relationship with God, not the world's value system. If you try to find your identity in this world, you will never feel like you are enough, possess enough or have done enough. Yet, in Christ, we could never get any better. We are perfect and complete in Him. Take the time to read, study and memorize the ABCs. These biblical truths have the power to transform how you see yourself in a radically good way!

I am **ALIVE** with God.
"You were dead because of your sins and because your sinful nature was not yet cut away. Then God made you **ALIVE** with Christ, for He forgave all our sins." (Colossians 2:13, NLT)

I am **BLESSED** by God.
"Praise be to the God and Father of our Lord Jesus Christ, who has **BLESSED** us in the Heavenly realms with every spiritual blessing in Christ." (Ephesians 1:3, NIV)

I am a **CHILD** of God.
"But to all who believed Him and accepted Him, He gave the right to become **CHILDREN** of God." (John 1:12, NLT)

I am **DEAD** to sin.
"So you also must consider yourselves **DEAD** to sin and alive to God in Christ Jesus." (Romans 6:11, ESV)

I am **ETERNAL**.
"For we know that if the earthly tent we live in is destroyed, we have a building from God, an **ETERNAL** house in heaven, not built by human hands." (2 Corinthians 5:1, NIV)

I am **FORGIVEN**.
"I am writing to you, dear children, because your sins have been **FORGIVEN** on account of His name." (1 John 2:2, NIV)

I am **God's POSSESSION**.
"But you are a chosen people, a royal priesthood, a holy nation, God's special **POSSESSION**, that you may declare the praises of him who called you out of darkness into his wonderful light." (1 Peter 2:9, NIV)

I am **HOLY**.
"For God's will was for us to be made **HOLY** by the sacrifice of the body of Jesus Christ, once for all time." (Hebrews 10:10, NLT)

I am **IMPORTANT**.
"Give all your worries and cares to God, for **He cares** about you." (1 Peter 5:7, NLT)

I am **JESUS' FRIEND**.
"You are My **FRIENDS** if you do what I command." (John 15:14, NIV)

I am **KEPT** by God.
"Who are **KEPT** by the power of God through faith unto salvation ready to be revealed in the last time." (1 Peter 1:5, KJV)

I am **LOVED** by God.
"This is love: not that we loved God, but that He **LOVED** us and sent His Son as an atoning sacrifice for our sins. (1 John 4:10, NIV)

I am **MADE** in God's Image.
"So God **created** mankintd in His own image, in the image of God he created them; male and female He created them." (Genesis 1:27, NIV)

I am **NEVER** alone.
"Keep your life free from the love of money, and be content with what you have, for He has said, "I will **NEVER** leave you nor forsake you." (Hebrews 13:5, ESV)

Chapter 2

A Life That's
Growing Somewhere Good

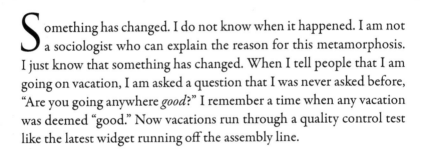

Something has changed. I do not know when it happened. I am not a sociologist who can explain the reason for this metamorphosis. I just know that something has changed. When I tell people that I am going on vacation, I am asked a question that I was never asked before, "Are you going anywhere *good*?" I remember a time when any vacation was deemed "good." Now vacations run through a quality control test like the latest widget running off the assembly line.

"Are you going somewhere tropical?"
"Are you leaving the country?"
"Are you flying somewhere?
"Is it expensive?"
"Did you get a good deal?"
"Will you see anything historic?"
"Will you hike up any mountains or raft any waves?"
"Are you going anywhere *good*?"

Vacations to Westerners have become like all of life—we want the biggest and best. Even if you plan a "relaxing vacation," make sure it has some palm trees within reach or a balcony with an ocean view. Anything less would be lame, boring, uninteresting—not good. Staying at home on a "stay-cation" to catch up on life is not socially admirable. If you want a real vacation that is deemed worthy of praise, then you must go somewhere, and it must be somewhere *good*.

As the author of this book, I am taking you on a vacation of sorts. I am the captain of this ship and for the short time we are together, you are my highly esteemed guest. So, you have the right to ask me up front, "Are we going anywhere *good*?" My answer is an unequivocal and confident "Yes!"

One of the most often quoted and memorized verses in the Bible is Romans 8:28, which just so happens to precede Romans 8:29, the verse we looked at in chapter 1. "And we know that in all things God works for the *good* of those who love him, who have been called according to his purpose." Read this verse over a few times before moving forward. Let the goodness of its truth go down deep into your soul. Believe me; this is better than a free cruise to the islands of the Caribbean!

God promises that in every situation and circumstance of life, He is working out good plans for those who love Him. He is planning something good for His children and doing so with great purpose. It is at this point too many Bible readers close the book, sit back, and breathe in the cool breeze saying, "Ahhh God is working all things for my good. How wonderful. Pass the piña colada."

Wait! Do not set sail yet. We have a major problem. Let me explain. You see, not everybody enjoys the same things. Not everyone really likes piña coladas or walking in the rain. Not everybody enjoys the same vacation. One person sees a camping trip as the greatest place on earth. They see the beauty of nature, the campfire at night, and the feeling of being out in the open among the wild as invigorating and exciting. Another person sees the same vacation and considers it a nightmare – the lack of good showers, the uncomfortable sleeping arrangements, and the constant battle of bugs and critters would make it more of a survival test than a vacation. We all do not enjoy the same things. We have our own personal preferences. We all have differing evaluations of what is deemed "good."

So when God says in His Word, "I am going to work everything out for good," you have to stop and wonder, "Whose good?" Is it the camping good or the Royal Caribbean type of good? Is it good in my book or good in my wife's book? Is this in-law good or me good? Whose good are we talking about?

The good God offers us is the *ultimate* good. It is the good that passes the test of time. It is the good that surpasses any cultural expectations or precedence. It is the good that goes beyond personal preference. It is the good that is not measured according to any finite man whose opinion and feelings can be fickle and fluctuating. It is the God ordained good. It is the good that God himself knows is best for us.

Were your parents the type of people who believed in corporal punishment? Three things I know hold true about corporal punishment. First, no kid likes it. Second, every parent says it hurts them more than it hurts the child. Third, kids do not buy number two, not even for a moment. Regardless of your feelings about spankings, in theory parents who exercise corporal punishment believe that in disciplining their child with a spanking or some other form of physical chastisement they are doing something to ultimately help the child in the long run.

When God says He is working all things together for our good, He is promising that He is working through every circumstance in life—the good, the bad, the pleasant, and the painful—for His good purpose. Now we know God is all-powerful and able to do the impossible, but we have to still ask another profound question. How can God take a tragedy and turn it into something good in the same way He takes a miracle and turns it into something equally good?

If I have a wonderful vacation, enjoying every moment and come back home refreshed, I can see how God is working all things for my good. If my Christian neighbor goes to the same vacation spot the following week and it rains the whole time, he gets food poisoning, and his kids drive him insane, how can that work for his good as well?

The answer comes from Romans 8:29, "For those God foreknew he also predestined to be conformed to the image of his Son, that he might be the firstborn among many brothers and sisters."

God's ultimate good in all of our lives is to make us more like His Son, Jesus Christ. In every circumstance and situation of life, God provides us with opportunity to grow into the wondrous nature of His Son, Jesus Christ. No trial is too hard and no victory too marvelous to stop God from using both highs and lows to work in us the Christ like nature He so lovingly desires to see molded into our lives.

If there was one thing God wanted more for you than any other it would be for you to become a model of His son Jesus Christ in your thoughts, attitudes, words, habits, behavior, relationships, and view of life.

Jesus Christ lived a full life here on earth. His divine nature did not limit His human experience. On the one extreme, Jesus faced the full gamut of trials, tribulations, and temptations. "For we do not have a high priest who is unable to empathize with our weaknesses, but we have one who has been tempted in every way, just as we are—yet He did not sin" (Hebrews 4:15).

On the other end of the spectrum, Jesus also experienced the incredible joys of love, friendship, the taste of good food, the invigorating feeling of a beautiful sunny day, and the warm fellowship with God his Father. Jesus experienced good, bad, and even indifferent days here on earth.

In all these experiences—the highs and lows, the ins and outs—the writer of Hebrews tells us that Jesus "did not sin." In other words, Jesus lived a fully pleasing life before God regardless of whether He had a good or bad day. It is this divine and wonderful quality of Jesus Christ that God declares is good in the purest sense of good.

Jesus Christ is God's perfect and complete representation of ultimate goodness here on earth.

So where does that leave us? It brings us to the conclusion that God's ultimate good for your life is not a destination. It is not a cruise line, an early retirement, fame, fortune or bulging biceps. God's ultimate goal for your life has more to do with your character than it does with your credentials. If there was one thing God wanted more for you than any other it would be for you to become a model of His Son Jesus Christ in your thoughts, attitudes, words, habits, behavior, relationships, and view of life.

Now we know that God's ultimate good is for us to become like Jesus. We also know that God is hard at work trying to accomplish this feat in our lives. So how does He do it? How does God take a vacation that is perfect and work it for my good, and take a similar vacation for my neighbor that is miserable and work it out for his good just as much as my own? I am so glad you asked.

My sons enjoy playing sports—any sports. Like all other kids, they have experienced the joys of winning and the frustration and pain of losing. At the end of the game, I am less concerned with whether they won or lost than "how-they-played-the-game."

Just the other day at my son Jordan's baseball game, one of his teammates struck out to end the inning. This little nine-year-old kid came huffing and puffing back to the bench throwing a major fit. It was embarrassing. He was using language that should never be known by a kid his age let alone be uttered from his chubby little lips. He threw his helmet, his bat, and his dignity all over the place.

The coach did the right job in addressing this little tike making him sit in the dugout for a good talk, and not allowing him to go back on the field. This little monster was not going to have anything to do with the coach's talk. He got up, stormed out the dugout, and headed off the field! At this point, his grandfather who was in the outfield headed down towards his grandson to intervene and stop the madness. "Get to the truck," were his only words spoken in public. I am hoping his words in private were as weighty as his Ford F-150. If anyone deserved a good round of corporal punishment it was this little brat—sorry, kid.

We do not hit every pitch in life for a home run. Sometimes we swing and miss. But whether we swing and miss or set the ball-a-sailing over the outfield fence, we all have a choice. Will we respond in a way that honors God and models the person of Jesus Christ? That is how God works everything for our good.

God works everything out for our good by providing us with the opportunity, power, and grace to live our lives in a manner of growing more Christ-like in character and behavior.

Our lives are a mélange of good and bad. Life can be bitter one moment and sweet the next. We can celebrate the birth of a newborn child in the morning and mourn the death of a loved one in the afternoon. We have sorrows and we have joys. We have exciting days and we have boring days. We write with ease in one moment and struggle with writer's block the next. One morning God feels as close as our cup of coffee, the next morning He seems to be gone on vacation. In every high and low of life, one thing remains constant – God is fully capable of using every life circumstance for our ultimate good of becoming more like His Son, Jesus Christ.

You cannot control the weather on your next vacation, but you can control the *whether*—whether or not your response to the rain honors God. You cannot control how your kid will act when he strikes out his next time at bat. You can choose to respond to his behavior in a way that mimics the person of Jesus Christ. We all have a choice in this matter. We have the choice to partner with God in His good work to make us more like His Son or to deviate from the course and go against His good plans.

In this, we learn the degree of our love for God. The person who loves God lives his life in a way that compliments and does not conflict with the plan and purpose of God to conform him to "the image of His Son."

Do you want God's ultimate good in your life? Do you desire to see His perfect plans come to fruition in your days here on earth? If the answer is yes, I invite you to continue with me on this journey as we break out the map of God's Word and discover God's good, pleasing, and perfect will for your life. It will be good!

Before you set sail with me, I want to make sure you have your ticket. The other day I was headed to a minor league baseball game with my entire family. The kids were packed in our minivan, the dog was in her crate, and the visions of hot dogs and cotton candy were dancing in our heads. Before I started my engine, something made me think to go back inside the house. I am glad I did. On my counter sat the tickets to the game. Without those little rectangular pieces of paper, I would have been driving my little tribe back home struggling to let my attitude be worked out for God's good! I am glad I got the tickets before I arrived at the destination.

Do you have your ticket? The ticket I am speaking of is not for the ball park, it is for another destination far grander and lovelier. It is the ticket to eternal life with God. It is the ticket to a vibrant relationship with your Creator. It is the ticket to the start of God's wonderful plan to work everything out for good in your life.

The ticket has one word on it, "SALVATION." And the good news is that God has paid for your ticket. You see, each of us has failed to be entirely good by God's standard because God's standard of good is Jesus Christ. You have been that brat, I mean kid, who has thrown the fit. You have been the jerk on the highway, at least once. You have been the one who has cursed another, stolen from someone, been envious, cruel, angry, jealous, covetous, greedy, pompous or immoral. You, I, we—the entire human race—have all lived our lives apart from the good and perfect plans God has for us. We have all sinned, that is, we have not lived perfectly like Jesus. In fact we have lived far from it.

So how do we clean up the mess we have made with our lives? How do we remove the marks of our sin from God's scorebook? How do we go from being guilty to being innocent? Can we just ask God to forgive us, will that do? God says it will not. In fact, God says that if you do the crime, you have to do the time. Here is how He puts it, "the wages of sin is death" (Romans 6:23a). When we sin, we deserve punishment. No good parent rewards a child's misbehavior with candy. Neither can a good, just, and loving God reward our sin with anything, but what it deserves. In God's estimation, sin is so severe that it deserves death.

But wait, there is good news! The verse continues, "For the wages of sin is death, but *the gift of God* is eternal life in Christ Jesus our Lord" (Romans 6:23). God does not want you to try and clean yourself up. It is a job you could never complete. It is like a home that has been destroyed by a hurricane. You cannot just do a little patch job and get on with life. You have to tear down what is left and start from scratch. God cannot just forgive your sins. He has to completely remodel your life!

God loved you so incredibly much that He sent His only Son Jesus Christ to this earth. Jesus did what we could not do. Jesus lived on this earth as a perfect, sinless human being. At the end of Jesus' life, He died on a cross as a way to pay for your ticket to be reconciled to God. Now God offers you the gift of eternal life, complete forgiveness, and total redemption through His Son.

Will you accept the free ticket of God's salvation found in the person of Jesus Christ?

Accepting God's gift of salvation is as simple as A, B, C. A stands for admit. Admit that you have sinned (fallen short of Jesus' perfection) and need God's forgiveness. B stands for believe. Believe that God loves you and sent His Son Jesus Christ to die on the cross for your sins (paid the price for your mistakes). C stands for confession (agreeing with God). Confess to God your need for His forgiveness and ask Him to make you into a new person.

You can accept and receive this free gift of salvation by praying a simple prayer. It is a prayer based on the three most polite phrases every parent teaches their child—Sorry, Thank you, and Please. The prayer goes something like this:

> *Sorry God, for the ways I have sinned against You. Thank You God, for sending Jesus to die on the cross for my sins. Please God, forgive my sins and come into my life. I want to follow You.*

32

If you have never prayed this prayer or one similar to it, I encourage you to slowly pray it through, make it your own, add what comes from your heart, and ask God for His forgiveness and a new lease on life. Accept the ticket of God's salvation and then hop on His Royal Cruise line. We are headed somewhere extremely good!

Remember These Truths and Take Action

- God promises that in every situation and circumstance of life, He is working out good plans for those who love Him.
- The good God offers us is the *ultimate* good to become like His Son, Jesus Christ.
- God works everything out for our good by providing us with the opportunity, power, and grace to live our lives in a manner that is growing more Christ-like in character and behavior.
- God freely offers you the gift of eternal life, complete forgiveness, and total redemption through His Son Jesus Christ. To receive this gift you simply Admit, Believe and Confess.

Personal Reflection and Group Discussion Questions

- How can every circumstance in life, good or bad, be used to help you grow more like Christ?
- How does God's *ultimate* good (to make you like Christ) compare to what you normally perceive as good?
- In what ways do you need to respond to seemingly bad circumstances in order to become more like Christ?
- Have you accepted God's free gift of eternal life offered through His Son Jesus Christ?

Meditation

God's ultimate good is for me to become like Jesus.

Prayer

*God, give me wisdom and power to make right choices
so I may become more like Christ.*

Bible References

- Romans 8:28
- Romans 8:29
- Hebrews 4:15
- Romans 6:23

Chapter 3

The Four Seasons of Christian Growth

G rowing up, people would say how they loved the four seasons of Upstate New York. I was confused. I only counted three. There was winter, recovery from winter, and preparation for winter. I still remember one Halloween having to wear moonboots over my costume so I could trek through the snow as I went from house to house. Somehow the scariness and fright of a Halloween costume is lost when you are forced to wear winter boots by your Mom, especially moonboots!

If I could control the weather, I would make it sunny, eighty-five degrees, with a mild breeze every single day, no exception. I do not think I would get sick of it. If I had my choice of a vacation, it would be somewhere equally warm and sunny. I am sure Alaska is beautiful, but I have no interest in going. I will be fine just looking at the pictures. What can I say? I am a sunny, warm weather kind of guy. It is just my personal preference, what I deem as *good*.

As much as my personal preference is for the summer months, I can appreciate God's handiwork and majesty in every season. The spring provides a sense of new life and hope. The flowers begin to blossom and the birds begin to chirp again. The wonderful array of fall colors is a natural mosaic that turns the world into an art gallery. If I am on a pair of skis, I can even appreciate winter.

As God has created four seasons in the world, He has also created four seasons in the life of His children. The seasons of Growing Up, Growing Out, Growing Deeper, and Growing Together make our world as Christians more colorful, delightful, and interesting than just having one season throughout our lives, even if it were eighty-five and sunny. In every season, God's overall purpose is to develop Christ-like character within us. The aspect of Christ's character God is developing varies with each season.

Jesus rebuked His contemporaries for being able to accurately predict the weather forecast, but not being able to understand the spiritual times and seasons they were in.

> *He said to the crowd: "When you see a cloud rising in the west, immediately you say, 'It's going to rain,' and it does. And when the south wind blows, you say, 'It's going to be hot,' and it is. Hypocrites! You know how to interpret the appearance of the earth and the sky. How is it that you don't know how to interpret this present time?"* (Luke 12:54-56)

Jesus' words were addressing the broader spiritual seasons and times affecting all people on earth, but the same principle holds true in our own personal lives. We miss out on God's best when we are unable to discern the season of life God has us in individually. Right now, you are in a spiritual season of life in which God is working to make you grow. Do you know what season you are in?

Growing Up

**When God has a person in a season of Growing Up,
they become consciously aware of their own sin, lack of
maturity, and need to change their attitudes, words,
and behavior to be like Christ.**

Growing Up seasons are often the toughest, hardest seasons of life. They are the winter so to speak. In these times, we are learning what it means to die to ourselves, our wants, our desires, our passions, and even our personal "rights." We learn how to give of ourselves to others and not look for anything in return.

Life transitions are another common means God uses to grow us up. We become a parent. We go off to college for the first time. We take on a new job that seems over our head. We need to take care of elderly parents. In all of these transitory moments, God is working to mature us and develop our faith in Him. We learn how to depend on God and trust in Him when we are in an uncomfortable environment. We become amazed at what we can accomplish through His power working within us.

Trials and hardship are common means by which God grows us up. God uses the tough times of life for the purpose of making us "mature and complete lacking nothing" (James 1:4). In times of hardship, we become humbled, broken and aware of our weaknesses, sin, and utter dependence on the Lord. God uses these moments in which we are tender and bare to mold the shape of our hearts.

**An important distinction to make and understand is that not
every trial is brought by God, but every trial can be used by
God to cause you to grow.**

If you are fighting a terminal disease, it may require you to grow more mature as a person, but it would be a misdiagnosis to say God made you sick. Sickness is a result of living in a fallen, unredeemed world. God is looking to redeem, restore, and heal the world. Jesus came to make people whole, not sick. At the same time, God can use a person's sickness, financial hardship or any other trial to help develop and grow them into the image and likeness of Jesus who "learned obedience from what he suffered" (Hebrews 5:8).

If you are in a difficult season today and God is working to make you Grow Up, take heart. Remember His promise to work all things together for your good—the ultimate good of making you more like Christ. On the other side of this season, you will be a stronger, wiser, and spiritually healthier person if you give God permission to change your heart as you go through the trial. God will use this season to grow you up in a way that reflects the beauty and purity of Christ's character.

Growing Out

The pain and struggle of Growing Up is different from the discomfort found in Growing Out. In this season, God will move upon your heart to give you greater compassion and conviction to share His love with the world around you. As God calls you to Grow Out, He is working to break off the fears that hold you back from talking with unbelievers about God. God is also at work to soften your heart to the needs around you, and move you beyond the places of passivity, complacency, indifference, and self-centeredness. If Growing Up is the winter of life, then Growing Out is the summer—a time to get out there into the world!

Jonah is a good example of a man God was intently working on to Grow Out. God looked upon the people of Nineveh with compassion and mercy. Jonah looked upon them with contempt and scorn. God saw an opportunity and believed the people of Nineveh could be transformed. Jonah looked upon the same people and saw no hope or desire for the people to change. Jonah needed to Grow Out!

Jesus often stretched the disciples to Grow Out of their comfort zone. After a long day of ministry to a large crowd of people, the disciples thought it best for everyone to depart to the nearest city so they could buy themselves something to eat. They asked Jesus to break up the crowd and send people on their way, a reasonable request. The disciples saw the situation through rational eyes. Many hungry people plus no food equals many hungry people. Jesus saw the people through eyes of compassion. Many hungry people with nothing to eat means we must find something to feed them.

The contrast between God's view of humanity and His plan of redemption is often miles away from our own comfort zone of extending a helping hand to others. The heart of Jesus is to reach out and extend beyond what is reasonable or comfortable.

> *You have heard that it was said, 'Eye for eye, and tooth for tooth.' But I tell you, do not resist an evil person. If anyone slaps you on the right cheek, turn to them the other cheek also. And if anyone wants to sue you and take your shirt, hand over your coat as well. If anyone forces you to go one mile, go with them two miles. Give to the one who asks you, and do not turn away from the one who wants to borrow from you.* (Matthew 5:38-42)

Viewing the world through Jesus' eyes transforms us. We go from being greedy to being generous, from pre-occupied to considerate, self-centered to other-centered, driven by our own passions to being led by God's compassion.

The sunny season of Growing Out requires us to put on a new set of shades so we see the world as Jesus sees it. The season of Growing Out calls us to extend our arms wide, as Jesus did on the cross, so others in need of God's grace and love can receive it through us.

Growing Deeper

I have a small garden in my backyard where my kids and I plant a variety of vegetables each spring. My daily work life is quite sedentary. I sit behind a computer much of the day, so it is a good change of pace to get my hands dirty and dig deep into the soil of God's green earth. In the Growing Deeper season of our lives, God is interested in us getting our hands dirty and having the roots of our faith grow deeper and stronger in Him.

Jesus gave a parable about a man who planted seeds. Some of the seeds landed on a path of uncultivated soil. Some of the seeds were picked up and eaten by the birds. Other seeds landed on some hard ground, maybe a sidewalk or brick patio. Lacking the necessary moisture, these seeds soon withered and died. Other seeds fell upon thorny ground and eventually were choked out by the neighboring weeds. Some of the seeds were fortunate enough to land on good soil and grew into a good crop that multiplied a hundred fold.

Our life and faith are tender and precious gifts from God. Our faith is rooted in God's Word, the ultimate seed of life. Our hearts are the ground in which God plants His Word. If your heart is softened and receptive to the Word of God, your faith will grow deeper and stronger. If your heart is calloused or cluttered with the cares of this world, the desire to be rich or a longing for the pleasures of this world, you will not bring forth good fruit and eventually your faith may wither away or even die out.

God's will for your life is to grow deeper in faith, love, and commitment to Him. As you daily read and meditate on His Word, God will make your faith stronger and grow your roots deeper. A tree that has deep roots is more apt to stand against the storms of this life. A tree with shallow roots will be susceptible to the inclement weather of life's circumstances and Satan's ploy to steal, kill, and destroy.

Growing deeper in God does not come about solely through His Word, but also through His Holy Spirit. Trees need water to flourish and prosper. Our spirits need the refreshing power of the Holy Spirit.

The power of the Holy Spirit living within gives us the strength, energy and love to live for God and grow deeper with Him.

Jesus stood and said in a loud voice, "Let anyone who is thirsty come to me and drink. Whoever believes in me, as Scripture has said, rivers of living water will flow from within them." By this he meant the Spirit. (John 37b-39a)

And this hope will not lead to disappointment. For we know how dearly God loves us, because he has given us the Holy Spirit to fill our hearts with his love. (Romans 5:5, NLT)

The two internal signs indicating God has you in a season of Growing Deeper are a hunger for God's Word, and a thirst for more prayer and worship.

God is cultivating our hearts to go deeper with Him by stirring up our passion for the knowledge of Him, but also the experience of His presence and manifestation of the Holy Spirit in our lives. If you find yourself hungering and craving after God, His Word, and the Holy Spirit's presence, you are likely in a season of Growing Deeper with God.

The Lord wants you to draw closer to Him, to love His Word, to be intimate in conversation with Him, and to hear His voice.

So that Christ may dwell in your hearts through faith. And... that you, being rooted and established in love, may have power, together with all the Lord's holy people, to grasp how wide and long and high and deep is the love of Christ, and to know this love that surpasses knowledge—that you may be filled to the measure of all the fullness of God. (Ephesians 3:17-19)

Growing Together

What makes the fall season beautiful is not one leaf, but the multitude of leaves that together make up a beautiful tapestry for our eyes to enjoy. One life is like one leaf. Many lives together are like the foliage of fall making the body of Christ full and beautiful. In the season of Growing Together, God is working on our hearts to draw us closer to our brothers and sisters in Christ. In this season, you feel compelled to develop deeper friendships with other believers with the hope of growing stronger in faith.

Growing Together is a season that encourages us through the mutual support of fellow likeminded believers in Jesus. We give and receive God's love by ministering to each other. God uses this season of Growing Together to build us up and make us healthier as a spiritual body and as a family. We encourage one another, love one another, pray for one another, and care for each other in our times of need. By Growing Together, all the body becomes healthier, stronger, and more vibrant.

Growing Together calls us to make disciples of one another, teaching each other what we have learned, "until we all reach unity in the faith and in the knowledge of the Son of God and become mature, attaining to the whole measure of the fullness of Christ" (Ephesians 4:13). As we work together and spend time with one another, we all as a whole become more like Christ in our character.

Polarized Christians are an endangered species. Therefore, God uses the community of believers to not only mature His body, but also to protect it from deception.

Then we will no longer be infants, tossed back and forth by the waves, and blown here and there by every wind of teaching and by the cunning and craftiness of people in their deceitful scheming. (Ephesians 4:14)

Every leaf has two sides, and the season of Growing Together likewise has two components. The first side is the edification and building up as mentioned above. The second side is the pruning and clipping away of what is not edifying and loving from our hearts. In the season of Growing Together, God will bring about conviction regarding how we treat other members of His family with our words, accusations, actions, and at times our inaction or lack of response.

God is not out to condemn us, so beware of the incriminating voices of Satan that tell us we have not done enough to please God. God is not pleased by our *doing*, but by Christ's *dying*. Yet He will convict us of our sins—both the wrongdoing and the good left undone.

In our season of Growing Together, we each become challenged to love people where they are, and to speak God's truth even when it may hurt.

> *Instead, speaking the truth in love, we will grow to become in every respect the mature body of him who is the head, that is, Christ.* (Ephesians 4:15)

What Season Are You In?

Is God primarily working to mature you and grow you up? If so, you may be in the winter season of **Growing Up.**

Are you feeling compelled to reach out to people around you or even people far away with the love of God and hope of the Gospel? If so, welcome to the summer season of **Growing Out.**

Is God moving on your heart to draw you closer to Him? Do you have an increased appetite to read His Word and be with Him in prayer and worship? If that is the case, you are likely in a season of **Growing Deeper** with God.

Is God moving on your heart to spend more time with other believers, to join a church, accountability group, small group or home fellowship? In this case, you are likely in a season of **Growing Together**.

Once you identify the season you are in, you can determine how you must dress for that season. Just like my Mom made me wear moon-boots on that cold, wintery Halloween, God wants you to dress appropriately for the weather of the season you are in. It would not be wise to wear flip flops in the snow or a winter coat in a hundred plus degree weather. As a loving parent, God wants you to "be thoroughly equipped for every good work" so that you may bear good fruit both "in season and out of season" (2 Timothy 3:17, 4:2). For the remainder of this journey together, we will explore in greater detail the four seasons of growth you will experience in life so that you can be fully equipped to bear good fruit!

Remember These Truths and Take Action

- Right now, you are in a spiritual season of life in which God is working to make you grow.
- When God has a person in a season of Growing Up, they become consciously aware of their own sin, lack of maturity, and need to change their attitudes, words, and behavior to be like Christ. Life transitions are another common means God uses to grow us up.
- As God calls you to Grow Out, He is working to break off the fears that hold you back from talking with unbelievers about God. God is also at work to soften your heart to the needs around you, and move you beyond the places of passivity, complacency, indifference, and self-centeredness.
- In the Growing Deeper season of life, God is interested in us getting our hands dirty and having the roots of our faith grow deeper and stronger in Him.
- In the season of Growing Together, God is working on our hearts to draw us closer to our brothers and sisters in Christ.

In this season, we feel compelled to develop deeper friendships with other believers with the hope of growing stronger in faith.

Personal Reflection and Group Discussion Questions

- What season of your spiritual life (Growing Up, Out, Deeper, Together) do you enjoy the most?
- What season of your spiritual life (Growing Up, Out, Deeper, Together) do you find the most difficult and challenging?
- What season of growth do you believe God has you in currently? Explain.

Meditation

God has me in a season of growth.

Prayer

God, no matter what season of life I am in, I want to grow with You.

Bible References

- Luke 12:54-56
- James 1:4
- Hebrews 5:8
- Matthew 5:38-42
- John 37b-39a
- Romans 5:5
- Ephesians 3:17-19
- Ephesians 4:13-15
- 2 Timothy 3:17
- 2 Timothy 4:2

Chapter 4

Larry and Harry

I had my first crush at an early age. Her skin was smooth and tanned. I loved putting my hands all over her. I was awakened by her beauty, and seemed to come alive in her presence. She was gorgeous in my sight, and I knew deep down within that I would spend the rest of my life with this amazing gift of creation. She was irresistible to me in every way, and she was truly lifeless without me. Who was this fascinating and wonderful beauty who captured my heart? Her name was basketball. Yes, I fell in love at an early age with the sport of basketball like no other thing on earth. To this day I cannot figure out why this simple game of hoops is still so fascinating and beautiful to me. Love is so blind.

It did not take long for me to figure something out about this game. The taller you got, the better you became. The old expression is true, "You cannot teach height." You can teach someone how to box out, how to shoot free throws, how to make a bounce pass, but you cannot teach someone how to be tall.

My parents were average height at best, so I knew that if I was going to be tall enough to play in the NBA—which was the only career I deemed worthy of life—it would take a miracle from the heavens.

**I was not overly interested in God as a kid, but I was
eager to be taller, and figured that if God truly did answer
prayer this was a good time to give it a shot. So I prayed.
I prayed that I would be six feet tall.**

Now at my young age, six feet tall was like a skyscraper in my mind.
In fact, no one in my whole family was six feet tall. It was the barrier
that had yet to be broken. It was the summit of the Eade family genes
and I was destined to reach it. Regularly, maybe even religiously, I
would secretly, but confidently pray to God, "I want to be six foot tall
when I grow up. Please help me to grow!"

Guess what God did. He answered my prayer. Today I stand six-
feet tall on the nose. Well, actually I am six foot tall on the top of my
head, but you know what I mean. Just think if I had had greater faith! I
mean imagine if I would have believed God to make me seven feet tall!
I would be signing autographs instead of writing books—a heck of a
lot easier. Six foot faith + Six foot prayer = Six foot man.

Ask yourself:

- *What level of faith do I have in God's ability for me to grow?*
- *Do I trust that God can turn me into a spiritual giant, a man or
  woman full of mighty faith?*
- *Do I set my eyes on something smaller, something tangible and
  realistic?*
- *Do I really believe that by the end of my life God will have
  worked His powers in me so mightily that people will compare
  my character to that of Jesus Christ?*
- *Am I settling for something manageable, more within my reach
  and not so high and lofty?*

It is time to step back behind the arc of your comfort zone and
shoot for God's absolute best and highest goal for your life. God's Word

says clearly that He wants you to be just like Jesus in your character. To be like Jesus is the highest of all spiritual goals one could accomplish. It is God's absolute will for every one of His children. It is for this reason we all need to Grow Up in a serious way!

In my childhood home we had a wall inside my parent's closet where we would mark how tall we were. We would stand as tall as possible with our necks stretched out high and our backs snuggly fit against this wall. A parent or sibling would come along and mark the top of our heads with a back and forth scratch of a pencil. We would turn around and compare it to the last mark, and write our name, the date, and age on the line. I would do this frequently.

"I have not grown taller since Wednesday. I will come back again in a couple days."

What can I say? I was eager to grow. Since I was the youngest of six kids, for the large majority of my life I was always looking up to other marks and names with envy and aspiration.

"I hope I make it *there* someday!" I would say as I looked up to my older brothers and sisters, not only in height, but also in permissions and activities.

When can I stay up that late? *When you get older.*

How long before I can drive a car? *When you are old enough.*

When can I spend your life savings by going off to a private four year college? *Son, your time will come!*

God sent Jesus Christ into this world to begin a new lineage of sons and daughters. Jesus is our Savior and Lord, but He is also our older brother and a model for us to follow after in this life. God's will for us is to become like Jesus so *"that he might be the firstborn among many brothers and sisters"* (Romans 8:29). God destines for us to look up to our big brother Jesus and aspire to reach His height in character, maturity, and lifestyle.

Take a moment right now and imagine a mark on the wall of life with your name written next to it. Now look further up the wall, way up higher than you are now and picture another mark that says the name of your older brother, "Jesus." This marks the spot of God's destiny for your life!

Early on in our Christian journeys we often have high aspirations and youthful eagerness. Our lives become unquestionably impacted by the love and grace of God, and this breath of new life inspires us to greatness. We believe God can do the impossible and that the supernatural is inevitable. No bar is too high, no mountain too steep, and no challenge too difficult. With God, truly all things will be possible.

As life goes on, we find out that changes do not necessarily come as easily as we had hoped at the start of our journey. We face personal setbacks. We get defeated by the same sin time and again. At some point we start to wonder if this amazing life God has in store for us is really that amazing at all.

Settling for Six-Foot Faith

That is when it happens. We begin to settle for six-foot faith. I think a lot of us are running on six foot faith. We see something that is just out of sight or maybe something that others have achieved. We set our eyes on it, and pray with some level of hope that God will make it true in our lives as well. It is not really something that is impossible for us and requires God. It is just something that we think would be nice to have, and if we can somehow get God's assistance, we would be pleased.

God's personal growth goal for us is so much greater than our six foot size faith. He honestly wants and believes that you and I can become perfect representations of His Son Jesus. In fact, God is committed to this goal.

For I am confident of this very thing, that He who began a good work in you will perfect it until the day of Christ Jesus. (Philippians 1:6 NASB)

God is not done with you, friend. He made dirt, and dirt don't hurt. Wait, that is not the right expression. God made you, and God don't make junk. That is much better. Yes, God has made you to be like Jesus Christ, and He promises in His Word that He will continue to work on you until you are perfectly like Him. **He wants you to be perfectly like Jesus!**

Remember that wall we had pictured in our brains a couple minutes ago (or thirty seconds ago if you are a fast reader)? Picture yourself standing against the wall with the name "Jesus" several feet higher than you. Now picture yourself against that wall slowly growing up, an inch at a time until you finally reach the mark of "Jesus" on the wall. The Bible says you are to grow inch by inch until one day you can see Jesus face to face. If God says you can do it, then you can do it. Now that you can envision it, start to believe it, for this is God's destiny for your life!

Conform to the Image and Likeness of Christ

If Jesus is the height we are after, what on earth does it look like to be conformed into the image and likeness of Christ? Measuring in feet and inches is something all of us can understand[2] and calculate, but how do we measure our character against Jesus? What does it mean to grow into the image and likeness of the Son of God?

Jesus gives us great insight into this benchmark that God has placed before us. In the one and only time in Scripture we find Jesus describing His personal nature and character, He states: "I am gentle and humble in heart, and you will find rest for your souls" (Matthew 11:29b). Jesus uses two words to describe His essence, His being, and His heart—gentle and humble. Let's grapple with these two words, and consider how they shape and reflect our spiritual growth and development.

True Humility

I worked with two guys in a corporate environment who both taught me lessons on being gentle and humble in their own unique ways. Larry and Harry were their names. No, this is not a joke or a

---

[2] If you happen to live in one of the few surviving countries that still makes use of the metric system, please note that six feet is equal to 1.8288 meters tall. See how much easier it is to use feet and inches! You know, it is not too late to change.

nursery rhyme. Larry and Harry did not walk into a bar together. Larry and Harry did not climb up a hill to fetch a pail of water. The names have *not* been changed to protect their identity either. We are talking about two real people by the names of Larry and Harry. I kid you not.

I met Larry when I was a summer intern working in a corporate office in New Jersey. Larry was in his early fifties. He was working as a contractor creating Access databases for the large pharmaceutical company that employed us both. We worked together for the entire summer.

Larry was a smart individual. He was also witty and had a good sense of humor. Most of all, Larry was humble and gentle. He was never boastful about himself, his accomplishments or his abilities. He was reserved and soft spoken. His focus was regularly on how other people felt, how they were doing, and their own needs. Larry was a sensitive and kind man who had genuine compassion and care for others, not the typical picture you get when you think of a corporate consultant.

I, on the other hand, was anything but humble. I was a young, cocky college kid in my early twenties who was faithfully working out in the gym and filled with as much testosterone as I was ego. Physically speaking, I was far stronger, muscular, and bigger than Larry. He had a thin, average build, and had never spent significant time in a gym or playing competitive sports. In size I was much bigger, but in character and class, Larry was a giant compared to me.

Being around Larry was an amazing blessing for me. In him, I saw a man who was more intelligent, skilled, and experienced than me without all the braggadocio and pride. Larry never made me feel inferior to him or beneath him even though I was a subordinate to him that summer. Instead, he was patient, kind, and willing to teach a big-headed jock like me how to do things on the computer that I never knew possible. Larry's lifestyle taught me what it meant to truly be meek and gentle at heart.

Then there was Harry. I met Harry in the same office building a few years later when I was wearing the badge of an official employee, no longer just a summer intern. Harry sat on the other side of my cubicle wall. We were cube neighbors. Working inside a glorified cardboard box has a way of humbling a man. You go from being motivated by your graduation commencement speech to working inside a convertible cardboard box—a serious serving of humble pie for anyone with high aspirations.

Now back to Harry. Harry is to this day one of the biggest men I have ever met in person. Harry had to be around six foot seven inches tall and weighed in at over 350 pounds (before he started Weight Watchers). He was a monstrous individual. He had the physique of an NFL offensive tackle. When you walked down the corridor and Harry was coming your way, you instantly felt small and insignificant. He was just that big. All my weightlifting and protein shake drinking were no match for Harry's natural girth and size. He was a monster.

Ironically, Harry had one of the most tender hearts and soft spoken voices you could find among men in our workplace. Similar to Larry, he was kind, courteous, and had a good sense of humor. On the wall of Harry's cubicle was tacked up a poster of the entire galaxy. The background of the picture was pitch-black and the poster was covered with small white dots representing stars, planets, and galaxies. Off to one side of the poster, not at all centered, was an arrow pointing to an infinitesimally small dot. At the other end of the arrow were the words, "You are here."

So here you have Harry, a man who is larger than life, intimidating by stature, and triple X large in size with a poster on his cube wall pointing to a nearly invisible dot that said, "You are here." Somewhere in life Harry he had come to the realization that as big as he was, he was small comparatively to the cosmos around him. The poster screamed one word to me: *humility.*

Jesus was the most gifted and strongest man to ever walk the face of this earth. He had all wisdom, all knowledge, and all power. He had every right and privilege to walk around with great confidence and boastfulness for His talent, skill, and outstanding resume of miraculous achievements. If anyone in human history had the right to be proud, it was Jesus, the Son of God and Creator of all mankind. All of Jesus' accomplishments, accolades, and abilities gave Him plenty of reason to boast. Yet, in spite of His prowess, position and power, Jesus chose to humble Himself. The Apostle Paul may have penned the most poignant and beautiful description of the character and person of Jesus in his letter to the church at Philippi.

> *In your relationships with one another, have the same mindset as Christ Jesus: who, being in very nature God, did not consider equality with God something to be used to his own advantage; rather, he made himself nothing by taking the very nature of a servant, being made in human likeness. And being found in appearance as a man, he humbled himself by becoming obedient to death— even death on a cross!* (Philippians 2:5-8)

Paul gives us a window into the soul of our Lord and an exhortation to follow His example. True humility starts internally. It begins as a mindset. It is a choice of posture that starts inwardly in our view of God, others, and the world around us. Then it shows itself outwardly in our character and behavior.

True humility does not deny one's positive, good or admirable qualities and characteristics. If you are intelligent, humility does not mean you walk around saying you are stupid. If you are good looking, you do not have to consider yourself ugly. If you are a good athlete or a wonderful mother, you do not need to consider yourself a slug or second class parent. Larry was great with computers and for him to say so would not have been boastful, it would have been true. Jesus himself said, "I am humble." Was He boasting of His humility? No, He was simply speaking the truth about Himself with confidence.

True humility acknowledges what makes us unique and special, but gives all the credit and glory back to God.

Jesus proved Himself humble and validated His testimony by His willingness to leave the comforts of heaven and take on a human body. He lived a humble life. He submitted to His human, imperfect parents. He spent the majority of His earthly life working the laborious, hands-on carpentry trade of His human father waiting patiently for the calling from His Heavenly Father to start His ministry. He chose to be the lowest of servants instead of the highest of royalty. He lived without a roof over His head, and asked other people for basic essentials like a drink of water. He sought to put other people's needs before His own. He was willing to set aside His own agenda and plans to compassionately bring restoration to others. At the end of His life, the culmination of His narrative on this side of heaven, Jesus' self-evaluation, "I am humble," was proven true by His selfless death on the cross for our sins.

If we are to follow in Jesus' footsteps and grow into His character, we must make the choice of humbling ourselves before God and before man. Humility is not optional for any Christ follower. Jesus taught His disciples, "Very truly I tell you, no servant is greater than his master, nor is a messenger greater than the one who sent him" (John 13:16). If our Master is a humble servant, then we must follow His lead and be humble servants ourselves.

The school principal who walks the hallways of her school and is willing to bend over and pick up debris from the floor is the model for the subordinate teacher who approaches a piece of scrap paper on his journey to the teacher's lounge. The loving Savior who was willing to humble Himself even unto death to put others first has set the example for all those who call Him "Lord."

The paradox of spiritual growth is that the lower we go, the higher we grow.

Jesus set the bar incredibly low, "He humbled himself by becoming obedient to death— even death on a cross." If our goal is to one day stand as tall as Jesus and see Him face to face, then the first step is to humble ourselves before God and before man.

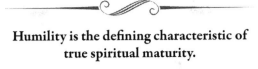

**Humility is the defining characteristic of
true spiritual maturity.**

The only way we will grow to be like Jesus is if we first humble our-selves as Jesus did, and seek to live a life of service to God and man. The Scriptures bid us to humble ourselves under God's control and power so that He may lift us up in His perfect timing (James 4:10, 1 Peter 5:6). In the same way that I prayed as a child for God to make me taller, now as a child of God I pray for God to make me smaller because I know that the lower I go, the faster I grow.

The whole purpose behind humbling ourselves is to allow Christ to live more vibrantly through us. It is not to demean ourselves and put ourselves down, but to make room for Christ to be glorified in our lives. An empty glass has room to be filled, but a full glass has no such room. Likewise, if we are full of ourselves, we cannot at the same time be full of Christ. John the Baptist said it most succinctly, "He must become greater; I must become less" (John 3:30).

When the disciples asked Jesus who was the greatest in the kingdom of heaven, He did not call upon a scholar, professor, doctor or rabbi as His model. Instead He called forth a child from the crowd and had that child stand before Him. He said spiritual greatest would require a con-version of heart to make us each childlike in nature and then went on to explain, "Whoever then **humbles himself** as this child, he is the greatest in the kingdom of heaven" (Matthew 18:4 NASB emphasis added).

If you have not noticed, young children are generally more open to being taught and learning than adults or even adolescents who seem to know it all. It is for this reason that our spiritual growth begins with humility. Humility admits, "I do not know it all. I have not arrived. I truly need to grow!"

If we are ever to grow spiritually mature, we must have a
teachable spirit. We must have an openness to see our faults,
failures, sins, and weaknesses. Then we must humbly
look to God for His grace to overcome and mature.

Ask Yourself:

Am I willing to humble myself before God and ask Him to teach me?
Am I willing to take on the mindset of a small child?
*Am I willing to look to my heavenly Father and pray that He will
make me taller in Jesus?*

Picture that chart once again and the mark on the wall with Jesus'
name. Instead of trying to get on your tippy toes to reach Him, get on
your knees and humble yourself before God asking Him to help you
Grow Up.

Remember These Truths and Take Action

- Jesus uses two words to describe His essence, His being, and
  His heart—gentle and humble.
- True humility does not deny one's positive, good or admirable
  qualities and characteristics. True humility acknowledges
  what makes us unique and special, but gives all the credit and
  glory back to God.
- If we are to follow in Jesus' footsteps and grow into His character, we must make the choice of humbling ourselves before

God and before man. Humility is not optional for any Christ follower.

- The paradox of spiritual growth is that the lower we go, the higher we grow. Humility is the defining characteristic of true spiritual maturity.

Personal Reflection and Group Discussion Questions

- If you had to choose two words to describe your own character, what would they be?
- Who is someone you know who demonstrates genuine humility and/or gentleness?
- What does humbling yourself before God or man look like?

Meditation

Jesus is humble and gentle at heart.

Prayer

God, make me humble and gentle like Jesus.

Bible References

- Romans 8:29
- Philippians 1:6
- Philippians 2:5-8
- John 13:16
- James 4:10
- 1 Peter 5:6
- John 3:30
- Matthew 18:4

Chapter 5

Nairobi. Nairobi. Nairobi.

I was to lead my first mission trip to Kenya, Africa with five other guys in tow. I had been to the continent of Africa twice before, once to Kenya and my second time to Ghana. Now it was my turn to lead a trip and I was excited for the opportunity. In the initial stages of preparing for the trip, "Trusting God" emerged as the focus and theme for our team. We worked on the concept of trusting God throughout all our sermons, our skits, and our prayers. Trust was particularly essential for me to lead a group of other men, most of whom were older than me, to another part of the world on a mission trip. I am sure the other guys felt the same and even greater need for trust in order to follow a young guy like me!

Our first flight was to London, Heathrow Airport. We had a quick layover before boarding our next flight to Nairobi, Kenya. After arriving in London, we were escorted through the fast lane of the security checkpoints in order to make our next flight on time. Once the six of us all got through the metal detectors without beeps and bells, we gathered in a huddle to regroup and head to our next gate. At this point, we were running behind schedule and the flight to Nairobi was already boarding.

As we scurried down the hallway, one of the fellow missionaries informed me that another guy on the team, Johnny,[3] went to the bath-

---

[3] To save our friend some face, I decided to choose an alias name of Johnny, short for Johnny-come-lately.

59

room and would meet us at the terminal. My first thoughts were, "Couldn't he hold it?" My gift of mercy was gushing forth. We took an elevator down one level to reach our next destination. From there we waited on a platform for a subway that would escort us to our terminal. A clock in the station displayed the number of minutes before the next train would arrive. I started calculating the minutes. If it will take three minutes more for the next train to arrive and Johnny is nowhere in sight, then it will be at least six minutes before he arrives at the gate. It was going to be tight!

The train arrived and we hopped in—a six pack shy one can. We jumped out of the train and headed up an escalator. Heathrow is a labyrinth I tell you! We reached the top of the escalator and there stood a British Airways stewardess wearing the cute little sailor's hat they wear, announcing aloud, "Nairobi. Nairobi. Nairobi."

I said to her, "Yes, we are headed to Nairobi."

Immediately she turned around and started booking down the hallway. We did what seemed most logical and started to run after her following after the clock, clock, clock sounds of her high heels as she raced down the terminal corridor. We arrived at the gate out of breath and feeling a sense of urgency and concern.

I spoke to the three workers at the counter saying, "We are a group of six. Five of us are here and our sixth member is on his way. He will be here any minute."

The crew insisted that we go and find our seats and they would wait for the last group member. I found my aisle seat and put my luggage in the overhead bin. I could not help but keep looking down the aisle waiting to see the head of our missing member pop around the corner onto the aircraft. I felt like a parent who momentarily loses a child. After a few minutes passed, I heard the sound of the overhead air being turned down. It was a sound that I recognized as a sign we were getting ready to taxi. Then I heard the mechanical sound of the plane door being shut to the aircraft—another noise that is indicative of a soon departure and one that would not permit anyone else to board the plane!

I stopped the nearest stewardess from going down the aisle, "Excuse me ma'am, but we are still waiting for one more passenger."

In a polite, British accent she replied, "I am sorry sir, but he will not be making this flight."

After the color returned to my face and my heart began to beat again, she assured me that she would provide any and all information about the next flight he would be on. There I was, leader of my first mission trip, and I had already lost one team member before we even arrived to our destination! Not a great start!

At that moment, by God's grace, the only words that came out my mouth were the very words God wanted to hear, "I trust you, Father."

The humility of Jesus began well before He was born into this world. Jesus made the humble choice of coming to earth as a missionary to humankind. Stepping down from His throne of authority and power, He embodied flesh and blood and chose to live in the world He created.

In accepting the venture of His mission to earth, Jesus surrendered His control and put His entire trust in God the Father.

Now, as our model for life and godliness, Jesus calls us to follow His example of faith and trust in God. Jesus modeled for His followers an unwavering trust in God the Father. Time and again we read in the Gospels of Jesus' faith and trust being lived out. Trust was the basis of many of His teachings and prayers. His life permeated a message of trust back to His Heavenly Father on a constant basis. "I trust you, Father" was not just a trivial, empty slogan, but a way of life that Jesus walked out daily before His followers. Regardless of how bad and daunting the circumstances seemed, Jesus firmly trusted God.

Put yourself in Jesus shoes, pardon me, sandals, for a moment and imagine the night of prayer He spent alone with God praying about which men to choose as His disciples. Jesus tuned His ears into His Heavenly Father's radio frequency to receive the Father's choices. If it were any of us, we would be thinking along the lines of Ivy League candidates in selecting the twelve guys who would support us. We would want the best, brightest, most mature individuals on earth to accompany us in this spiritual journey. Being on a mission to save the world is a tad bit more important than the NFL draft. We would want the best picks!

Do you remember in elementary school gym class when they would have two captains picking their individual teams? The worst feeling in the world is being the last person picked. You feel like the runt of the litter, the one nobody wants. In God's economy, the last are first and the first are last. The Father sent the message down to Jesus to pick out twelve guys who had no ministry experience, had bad tempers, ego problems, doubts, fears, and one who would ultimately betray Him. Jesus completed His night in prayer and did not doubt the Father's directive for a moment. He moved forward in trust.

It is time for a true confession. I do not know about you, but for me trust is easy. Yes, trust is easy when things are going my way, opportunity just cannot stop knocking at my door, hope is on a high, and everything is moving forward. In these times, I can confidently boast, "I trust in God." Honestly, trusting God in good times does not take much faith. Real trust and faith in God is not proven in the best of times, but rather in the worst.

Trust is like a parachute. You need it the most when you feel like you are falling to the ground without any support.

Jesus had that type of trust. The disciples were about to learn this lesson as they are out in a boat. Suddenly they find themselves out in the middle of the lake with the wind blowing, the waves crashing, and the water coming into the vessel in bucket loads. They start freaking out. All the while, Jesus is catching a cat nap in the stern of the boat.

Sorry Jesus, you need to roll up your little carpet because naptime is soon to be over. The disciples awake Jesus saying, "Master, Master, we are going to drown!" (Luke 8:24). Jesus gets up, rebukes the wind and waves, and then rebukes His disciples for their lack of faith.

In hindsight it is easy to look at the disciples lack of faith and think, "Come on guys. Did you really think Jesus' life would end this way, in a storm? Don't you know that you are part of a much bigger story?"

It is so much easier to critique the disciples' lack of faith than it is to examine our own, but stop for a minute and ask yourself:

- *Do I ever feel like there is no hope?*
- *Do I ever feel like God has fallen asleep on me?*
- *Do I ever wonder if God is aware of what is going on in my life?*

We all face doubts. We all have concerns. We all lack trust from time to time. Jesus knew this and counseled His disciples, "Don't let your hearts be troubled. Trust in God, and trust also in me" (John 14:1 NLT). The troubles we experience are not just ones of outward expression; they are an internal struggle of the heart. God wants our hearts, our minds, and our very souls to be embedded in trust. He will even allow our life's boat to be shaken and tossed about for the purpose of building our trust. Truthfully, we are just as secure in the storm as we are on the shore.

**Even when our trust in God wavers,
God is not wavered by our lack of trust.**

Make a declaration today. Say it out loud. "I trust you, God." Now repeat it with confidence until you mean it with all your heart. "I trust you, God." Words like these bring joy to the Father's heart.

Early on in my Christian journey, my trust in God was as stable as the disciples' boat while the waves crashed against it. If circumstances did not turn out as I had hoped or expected, I looked to God with anger and disappointment. I have shaken my fist towards heaven more times than I would like to admit. Over time, my trust has become stronger as I have witnessed God's faithfulness. It is becoming a bedrock and foundation upon which my heart can rest in peace.

You will keep in perfect peace those whose minds are steadfast, because they trust in you. (Isaiah 26:3)

If we are to grow in Christian maturity and become more like Jesus Christ, we must learn to trust God in all circumstances and at all times. Building trust takes time, but it also takes a decision on our part. We must decide now before all hell breaks loose that we will trust God in every aspect of our life. It is a bit late to figure out if you are going to trust God when you are in the midst of a storm.

It is so much better to determine your position of confidence and trust before the ship sets out to sea.

I am thankful that our theme for the mission trip I led was trusting God. It set a foundation for me that allowed me to respond to my circumstances in faith instead of doubt, fear or even anger. My pre-determined heart position was dialed into the place of trust. In that moment when the cabin doors were closed and we were shy one missionary from the plane, I was able to say, "I trust you, Father." I knew this was only a test of faith. In my heart of hearts, I truly believed God would work this situation out for His *ultimate* good.

Remember, the ultimate good is for us to become like Jesus Christ, not for us to make every flight or to never have turbulence. Sometimes it takes a missed flight or a shaky one to test our hearts and truly find whether our trust is in God or in our circumstances. The ultimate good for the disciples was not that they got to shore safely. Instead, it was that they encountered a new aspect of Jesus' character in which they would one day be able to model themselves. Their experience provided a portal for Jesus' followers throughout the ages. We can now take the example of faith demonstrated to us by Jesus and walk in the same degree of trust in our own personal lives. It is an encouragement for us to grow up into Christ's level of pure trust, even when life gets stormy.

As we neared the Nairobi airport, the same stewardess came by my seat with a small message on a piece of paper. Sent from the ground, to the pilot and printed out in his cabin, (Who knew they had a printer in the cockpit?!), was a slip of paper with a cryptic message explaining how Johnny would be on the same flight to Nairobi at the same time the next night. He was going to be twenty-four hours late.

I took a deep breath, thought for a moment about how to lead at this juncture, and prepared myself to tell the rest of the team who were seated in various places on the plane. They did not even know we were missing Johnny. The plane touched ground and we walked off the plane onto the runway, and then took a bus to the nearest terminal to pick up our bags and go through security.

I explained to the guys what had happened and how this was just a test for us to trust God. I also made everyone agree that we would show mercy and grace to our fellow brother. We committed to honor him and also keep a tight lid on all our potty jokes at least for a couple days until this blew over and Johnny felt "relieved." Meanwhile back in the Heathrow airport, Johnny was getting himself ready to spend the night rolled up on a bench inside the terminal awaiting his flight the next day.

We have the luxury of reading the stories of Jesus in hindsight. For many of us, we have read the feeding of the five thousand so many times that it has somewhat lost its wonder. We can read the miracle at Cana where Jesus turned water into wine so matter-of-factly that we do not consider the implications for our own life. Peter walking on water gets reduced down to a pat expression, "We must step out of the boat" instead of becoming a terrifying and exciting moment in which we hold on to the boat's edge for dear life. The stories have become too familiar.

Every day we face challenges. Some are relatively small and insignificant. We lock our car keys inside the car. We get a flat tire. We lose a document on our computer and cannot restore it. Not the end of the world, but a test of faith and trust to be sure. Other trials are more monumental and overwhelming to us. We lose our job or receive a bad diagnosis from the doctor.

In those moments, God is providing us with an opportunity. The opportunity is for us to take what we know from the Scriptures and apply it directly to our circumstances today. The woman loses a coin and then finds it; I lose my keys and believe they will be found. Jesus calmed the storm on the Sea of Galilee, so I trust Him when my tire goes flat. Jesus healed various kinds of sickness and diseases; I will believe Him for my healing regardless of what the doctors predict to be possible.

**We must learn to trust God with an unshakeable faith
as if we have already read the end of the story!**

Two days after we arrived in Kenya, our fellow missionary was back with the team and we were headed to our first exploit and outreach the next day. Our plan was to travel to a small village in a remote area to provide the Pokot people with clean drinking water, interact with some school children, and play the Jesus film at night. After the film played, we would have one of our missionaries stand up and share a message to the crowd inviting them to accept Jesus as their Lord and Savior.

Johnny approached me in the afternoon and explained what took place while he was camping out in Heathrow, "I was in the coffee shop the next morning and saw a little boy there with his father. As I looked at the two together, God started to speak to me about the relationship between fathers and sons and I wrote down some notes. Can I review them with you?"

As I reviewed the message he had crafted, I realized it would be a perfect fit for our preaching that night after the Jesus film. Over a hundred people from this remote area showed up to watch the Jesus film outside a small school where we had ministered earlier that day. At the end of the movie, Johnny stood up before the crowd with his translator by his side to give the message he received while in the airport. Looking down at his crinkled notes which were being illuminated by the flashlight he held in his hand, he spoke of God's love for us, His children. He spoke about the important role parents play in their kid's lives. At the end of his message, he invited the listeners to raise their hands if they wanted to accept Christ into their lives and ask His forgiveness. One after another, hands began to reach high to the heavens until we counted over seventy children and adults with their hands raised to accept Jesus into their hearts and lives!

In hindsight, I am so glad that Johnny missed that flight! It was a great lesson for me in faith, trust, and belief in God's goodness and grace. God was truly working out this situation not only for our ultimate good, but for the eternal good of seventy plus souls who accepted Christ that night. It will be forever recorded in my mind as just one more miracle Jesus performed here on earth.

Are you ready to ask yourself some tough questions?
- *What is the level of my trust?*
- *Do I trust God when life seems to be on a fast track to nowhere?*
- *When I am running late, running out of money, running out of patience or running out of gas, do I trust God to be sovereign and in control?*

Let's challenge our understanding and faith one step further.
- *What if Johnny had stepped up to speak and his words fell on deaf ears?*
- *What if no one accepted Christ that night?*

- *What if his plane ride was delayed two days or more instead of one?*
- *What if the story did not have such a happy ending, could we still put our trust in God to be working all things for our good?*

Sometimes God works in the circumstances of our life in a way that is understandably good. In fact, everything that is perfectly good in our lives has its source in God, no exceptions. (James 1:17) Other times, we will experience grave disappointment. Living as a Christian does not exclude us from being tried and experiencing hardship. Jesus did not escape hardship and neither will we. In fact, He promised troubles would come to those who follow Him! "I have told you these things, so that in me you may have peace. In this world you will have trouble. But take heart! I have overcome the world" (John 16:33). The question is not what we will face, but how will we respond to what we face.

The question is not whether we will face trials in life. Trials are inevitable. The real question is how we will respond to the trials that come our way.

Jesus overcame the world and now empowers us to overcome it victoriously as well. "For everyone who has been born of God overcomes the world. And this is the victory that has overcome the world—our faith" (1 John 5:4, ESV). Remember, the ultimate good for each of us is to become more like Christ. To be like Christ means we learn to have an attitude of faith in spite of unfavorable circumstances.

It comes down to this one simple question. When life is turned upside down and you cannot see how things will turn out, will you, like Jesus respond in absolute faith, trust, and confidence before God? The choices we make on a daily basis to trust God regardless of our circumstances build in us the kind of mature faith that honors God and models Jesus Christ to the world around us.

Remember These Truths and Take Action

- In accepting the venture of His mission to earth, Jesus surrendered His control and put His entire trust in God the Father. As our model for life and godliness, Jesus calls us to follow His example of faith and trust in God.
- Trust is like a parachute. You need it the most when you feel like you are falling to the ground without any support.
- If we are to grow in Christian maturity and become more like Jesus Christ, we must learn to trust God in all circumstances and in all times.
- The ultimate good is for us to become like Jesus Christ (which encompasses trusting God entirely) not for us to make every flight or to never have any turbulence in life.

Personal Reflection and Group Discussion Questions

- Consider Jesus' journey to live on earth. How did this voyage require faith and trust in God?
- Think of a time when your faith and trust were really tested. How did you fair?
- What person do you know who exemplifies a life of faith and trust in God?
- What would it look like for your trust in God to grow dramatically? How would you live differently?

Meditation

I trust God who works all things for my good.

Prayer

God, teach me to trust You with all my heart.

Bible References

- Luke 8:22-25
- John 14:1
- Isaiah 26:3
- James 1:17
- John 16:33
- 1 John 5:4

Chapter 6

Save the Birds!

Over a period of a few years, some trees in my backyard had grown out of control becoming a breeding ground for weeds and vines. My small plot of land had grown into a mini jungle, an adequate home for Tarzan, but an unsightly blemish for east coast suburbia. So with electrical tools and clippers in hand, my oldest son Elijah and I went on a mission trip to our backyard. We forged together to cut back the forest that was steadily closing in on us. Little did we know what surprise we would find hidden within our trees.

As I was hacking down some shrubbery, I stopped to take a look at my progress as well as what was ahead. That is when my eyes latched on to a disturbing sight. Within an arm's length of my next slash of the rotating blades was a bird's nest. The woven assembly of twigs and twine was hanging sideways with one bird still inside the nest, one hanging off the edge and two more that had fallen on the ground.

Just one more swipe of my electrical clippers could have created a flurry of blood and feathers. I set my tool down, went over to my son who was busy snapping branches, and brought him over to the bird's nest. I have always had a soft spot for birds. My fatherly instincts rose up when I saw these cute, defenseless baby birds. Recognizing I had unsettled their home by my branch hacking, I felt a sense of obligation for these little creatures. My son Elijah is an all-out animal enthusiast, no matter what species or breed. His heart was equally compassionate for the chicks. We were both touched and our mission immediately shifted from chopping down trees to saving lives—bird lives.

After a quick brainstorm between us, and a feverish search on the Internet by Elijah to learn what he could about rescuing birds, we realized it would be obligatory to relocate the birds back into a safer location off the ground. We found a small basket lying around the house. Then we found some scrap wood and shredded paper and assembled these components together to create a brand new home for the four brother and sister birdies. We nailed the man-made nest up high on the closest tree trunk and prepared ourselves for the rescue of our fine feathered friends.

My son put on a pair of unused cotton gloves and carefully secured each bird in his hand, one at a time, and placed them into their new, no mortgage, paid off home—oh to be a bird! The save and rescue mission seemed to be near completion. Now came the moment of truth. Would the mother bird find her babies in their new home? More importantly, would she return to her flock after they had been handled by humans?

I stood away from the scene by a dozen yards or so and spent time cleaning up the branches. Meanwhile, I kept the relocated nest in the corner of my eye, hoping and praying for the mother bird to return. As I prayed and even pleaded for God to send Momma Bird back to her babies, I felt the impressions of the Holy Spirit upon my heart.

It is good to want these fledgling birds to be reunited with their mother and be made stronger. What about the fledgling people around you who are floundering in their faith and need to be strengthened?

As quickly as this thought came into my mind, the story of Jonah also rose up in my spirit. After being used by God to rescue a dying city of people, Jonah threw a major pity party. Jonah sat outside the city, camped out under the shade of a plant prepared for him by God and fell asleep. The next morning when he awoke, the plant was eaten away by a worm sent by the Almighty. Jonah sat burning with anger under the hot sun, frustrated and ticked off at God and life—all because of a plant that died.

God responded to Jonah's sulking and sour spirit:

"Is it right for you to be angry about the plant?"

"It is," he said. "And I'm so angry I wish I were dead."

But the Lord said, "You have been concerned about this plant, though you did not tend it or make it grow. It sprang up overnight and died overnight. And should I not have concern for the great city of Nineveh, in which there are more than a hundred and twenty thousand people who cannot tell their right hand from their left—and also many animals?" (Jonah 4:9-11)

Then Jonah replied back to God, no wait, Jonah never got the chance to reply back. Hey, that is not fair. No rebuttal by Jonah, no further explanation, no chapter five, that is it, end of story? I guess God's point was made clear.

God has a heart for people being saved more than any other thing on this beautiful earth He created—more than the whales, the pandas or even cute baby birds. God is on a mission to save people from their spiritual ignorance and bring them into a relationship with Him.

So there I stood, a pastor, preacher, Christian author and friend of Jesus, convicted by God when I had only planned to come and cut down a few trees. My thoughts went to all the younger Christians, even people who I had guided to put their faith in the Lord, who were floundering in their faith and as susceptible to Satan and his demons as birds fallen out of a nest would be to a squirrel, mouse or rat.

Do I really care like God cares? Furthermore, do I really care about the people who do not know Christ at all? How many people are there similar to the people of Nineveh that I simply avoid, because like Jonah I am not fond of them and cannot waste my time? Yet, God's heart is to seek and save lost people. His heart is to gather in the lost sheep. His heart is to reach out beyond what is comfortable to rescue people from the snares of sin and spiritual death. Do I really care like God cares? Does His mission resonate deeply in my own heart and keep me up at night?

If I am honest, if we are all honest, the answer would have to be a resounding, "No." Of course, we care some, but what level of care do we have and how does our care for lost souls compare with our care for other lost items in life – whether it be endangered species, the TV remote or our car keys? Let's go a step further and ask, "How does my level of care for lost people compare to Jesus' level of compassion?"

In Jonah's case, the compassion gauge was on "E." Jonah was more concerned with his own personal comfort than he was with God's agenda to seek and save a lost city of people. It seems to be a common epidemic in our day as well, even among God's own people who have been rescued out of the snares of sin and death themselves.

We are saved. We know it. Now let's move on to more important things, like building our retirement fund or maybe something more spiritual like building a new sanctuary for God's people. But when it comes to spending our time, energy, resources and even our life to seek lost people, too often we bail.

If we are ever going to grow into the image and likeness of God's Son, Jesus Christ, then we need to grow in our compassion for the lost, misdirected, ignorant, blind, hurting, sinful people who are distant from God. "For the Son of Man came to seek and to save the lost" (Luke 19:10).

The Heavenly Father's mandate for our lives is to go on a search and rescue mission for lost people and prodigal sons and daughters. This is our assignment whether or not we chose to accept it. Most Christian people do not have a problem acknowledging the mission of God to seek and save lost people. It is not a mental assent to a prescribed truth that we are lacking. We can all nod our heads and agree that God is into the business of saving lost people. That is typically not our problem. God wants to save the world. God is compassionate for people. Good for God. Let's hope He does a fine job doing it.

Our problem is not acknowledging God's side of the equation, like Jonah, it is having a compassion and personal commitment to go after the mission God has for us with enthusiasm, zeal, and joy. I mean, let's be honest here. If you hear about a social event at church with food, music and friends, you would be all in to join the party. In fact, you might cancel other obligations you have just to be able to enjoy the time with friends from church. On the other hand, if the church was organizing a day to do some door to door evangelism, you would find some *really* good reason not to attend "this time around."

"Oh, I am sorry, but it is our pet snake's birthday that day. We are all tied up, maybe next year."

Like Jonah, we slither away onto a ship headed as far from evangelism as the East is from the West. In fact, evangelism has become such a scary and loaded term, for the purpose of this book and in the hope that you will keep reading further, we will change the term from evangelism to "seeking." Because truly, seeking after people that God loves is really at the heart of our mission. We cannot save a soul even if our own soul depended on it. God truly is the only one who saves.

What we can do, is to go on a search and rescue mission *with* God to find people who do not know Jesus and simply make an introduction.

An introduction—that is a good way to look at it, and much less intimidating if you ask me. Don't you enjoy introducing people? I know I do. I especially enjoy introducing people who I believe will have a great connection and kindred spirit. Often times at church when I am telling someone about another person they really need to meet, "Vo*ilà*", the other person just happens to appear right around the corner. I just love providence.

All God is looking for us to do is to introduce people to Jesus. "Hello Sally, this is Jesus. He already knows you, but you don't know Him really well. Why don't you two spend some time talking about life?" An introduction is by no means a conversion. It is only a conversation. Remember, only God converts. We simply introduce. That does not sound too painful and scary, now does it?

This year for the first time I sent out an electronic invitation for my son's birthday party. It was a neat experience being able to see people's R.S.V.P. come through electronically. I love it when technology makes things work easier. An introduction to Christ can come in many forms as well. It may come as an invitation to church, or an invitation for a person to join you for a Christian concert. It may entail giving a person a good Christian book to read or sending them daily devotionals via email. Maybe you invite someone to join you for Bible study or just maybe, when the time is right, you invite them to accept Christ into their life. An invitation to follow Christ can come in many stages and forms; it is simply an offer, an extension of your hand to allow another person to grab onto the hand of Jesus. Be creative. Be bold. Invite others to take their next step to learn more about Christ and draw closer to Him.

As much as I enjoy introducing people, I also appreciate being introduced to people as well. In fact, that is how I met my wife. We worked in separate office buildings, for two companies about an hour's drive away from each other in the beautiful Garden State of New Jersey. We had co-workers who knew us both, one working with Amanda, the other with me. They also knew we were Christians and that we were single, so they thought it a good idea to introduce us. The rest is, as they say, history.

When my wife and I got married, Marc and Tatiana, the couple that introduced us, were overjoyed!

We all have a sense of delight when we make a positive contribution in someone else's life that alters their destination, direction, and future for the good.

We feel like we have accomplished something of true meaning and significance. That is exactly how Marc and Tatiana felt. They were overjoyed to participate in our story in such a significant and meaningful way. The greatest contribution you can ever make in this world is to introduce another person to Jesus Christ. No other good deed done on this earth can even come close to or compare to this honor.

God has given me the distinct privilege of introducing a good number of people to Jesus since I first met Jesus myself. I have had just as many and more people show no interest or even decline the invitation. But honestly, one person who willingly accepts Christ's offer of salvation is greater than ten thousand who reject it.

I tell you that in the same way there will be more rejoicing in heaven over one sinner who repents than over ninety-nine righteous persons who do not need to repent. (Luke 15:7)

At the end of the day, or more importantly at the end of this life, they are accountable for their decision to accept or reject the Savior. Our responsibility is simply to make a compelling offer and invitation.

That is what Jesus did. Jesus was constantly engaging people where they were at and asking, inviting, and even risking them to walk further with Him on the journey of life and eternity. Jesus saw two brothers, Simon Peter and Andrew, fishing on the shore.

"Come, follow me," Jesus said, "and I will send you out to fish for people" (Matthew 4:19).

The Bible says they got up immediately and followed Him. That is a pretty impressive response. Jesus kept walking along with His latest followers, Simon Peter and Andrew, when He spotted two more brothers, James and John, along with their Dad, Zebedee. He invited them to join Him on the journey and immediately they left their boat and their own Dad behind to follow Jesus. They dropped their careers, left their family ties, and followed Jesus without hesitation! Imagine that, four guys in one day decided to quit everything to follow Jesus. That is some good fishing!

Now wouldn't it be beautiful if you and I had the same charisma, love, and absolute brilliance of Jesus so that we could say to someone, "Drop everything you are doing today and make a commitment to follow Jesus Christ," and then see them immediately choose to follow Him? Wow, that would be wonderful! Okay, the dream is over; now let us wake up to reality. You and I both know that more often than not, it does not work that way. People can be indifferent, angry or hostile towards God Himself, without even mentioning the name Jesus. Maybe they do not insult you, but instead they say something to the effect, "I am glad you found what makes you happy. Good for you." Then they dismiss you in some patronizing, but polite way.

Here is the good news. Jesus faced the same type of rejection and even worse from people He invited on the journey. Take the rich, young ruler as an example. He chose earthly riches over eternal wealth. The Pharisees chose religious tradition over the power and love of God. How disheartening. Let's not forget the same Simon Peter who immediately dropped his net to follow Jesus was also the one to deny Him not once, not twice, but three times! Cock-a-doodle-doo!

So let's face the facts. Some people are going to be warm and receptive to your invitation and others will flat out reject it.

Whether they accept or reject your offer is really no skin off your spiritual back. It comes with the territory.

Some will say yes. Some will say no. Some will be indifferent. Some will need more time to think about it. **One thing remains the same; God loves them all.** What you and I need to be concerned with is whether or not we are giving and living a compelling invitation for them to want to follow Christ. God's grace is sufficient for us to do our part and trust Him with the rest.

If we are truly to live out our faith to a lost and dying world like Jesus did, we must interact with people in their everyday lives and build relationships with them. That is what Jesus did. In fact, not only did Jesus invite others to follow Him, He made it a point of being among people and hanging out with them. He ate and drank with common people and social outcasts, even at times inviting Himself over for dinner (Luke 19:5)! We cannot keep people at an arm's length if we are to embrace them with Jesus' loving invitation.

Drive-by Christianity just will not work. We need to get involved in people's lives and actually learn to like people for who they are, and believe God for who they can become.

My dream for those little birds to be all they could was about to become a reality. About fifteen minutes into my branch snapping, cutting and bagging, my eyes saw something that brought me great delight. It was the Momma bird! She found her little babies and came to see them in their new home. Looking at their new synthetic nest she thought, "You have done well for yourselves. I ought to leave you alone more often." She returned a second time with some food in her beak to drop down into the hungry mouths of her fledgling family.

I was pleasantly pleased and relieved. We saved the birds. They were rescued and redeemed. Only a few days later, they had the strength to fly the coup, leave the nest, pack their bags, and start their own journey of life for themselves. My son and I were able to save these birds from the hazards of the wild, but it was Momma Bird who nourished them, strengthened them, and then finally when the time was right, kicked them out of the house to live on their own. I guess that makes her an empty nester, literally.

How delightful and sweet to know they were saved and are now living on their own strength. Likewise, the Father is pleased when one person turns from their sins and turns or returns back to Jesus, and then gains the strength to live out their faith and even bring others to know the Savior themselves. It delights His loving heart.

My brothers and sisters, if one of you should wander from the truth and someone should bring that person back, remember this: Whoever turns a sinner from the error of their way will save them from death and cover over a multitude of sins. (James 5:19, 20)

Remember These Truths and Take Action

- God has a heart for people being saved more than any other thing on this beautiful earth He created—more than the whales, the pandas or even cute baby birds. God is on a mission to save people from their spiritual ignorance and bring them into a relationship with Him.
- If we are ever going to grow into the image and likeness of God's Son, Jesus Christ, then we need to grow in our compassion for the lost, misdirected, ignorant, blind, hurting, sinful people who are distant from God.
- Only God saves people, not us. What we can do is to go on a search and rescue mission with God to find people who do not know Jesus and simply make an introduction. The greatest contribution you can ever make in this world is to introduce another person to Jesus Christ.
- We need to get involved in people's lives, actually learn to like people for who they are, and believe God for who they can become.

Personal Reflection and Group Discussion Questions

- How does it feel when you find or rescue something that you had lost?
- If you had to rank your level of compassion on a scale from one to ten, one being low and ten being the compassion of Jesus, where would you put yourself today?
- Who are the people you know who need God and could use your help making an introduction?
- What priorities would need to change in order for you to prioritize God's heart for lost people?

Meditation

God desires all people to know Him.

Prayer

God, use me to introduce others to Your Son, Jesus Christ.

Bible References

- Jonah 4:9-11
- Luke 19:10
- Luke 15:7
- Matthew 4:19
- Luke 19:5
- James 5:19, 20

Chapter 7

Bold Love

As mentioned in the last chapter, my wife Amanda and I were introduced to one another by our co-workers. The first time we met was on a blind date along with Marc and Tatiana, the couple who introduced us. We met at a Lebanese restaurant in New Jersey with a fabulous name, "Pierre's Restaurant." Being Lebanese myself and having the name Pierre, I could not think of any better place for a blind date. What can I say, I like home field advantage!

Now the interesting thing about our little arranged meeting and date was that I had never seen a picture of my wife before meeting her. We met before the days when social media and smartphones made taking and sharing pictures so easy. I was only told by Marc that Amanda was attractive and that she was a Christian. Apart from the credibility of Marc's testimony and trust in his good taste, I was going purely on "blind faith" in God.

I can still vividly remember the first time my eyes laid hold of my future wife. I arrived early to the restaurant as did Marc and Tatiana. We sat at the table and had some small talk. Their backs faced the restaurant entrance, but I had a full view of everyone who came through the doors – a strategic move on my part.

That's when it happened. On the opposite side of the restaurant entered a tall, gorgeous woman in a red dress with white polka dots. I thought to myself, "I sure hope that's Amanda!" This woman in red proceeded to walk step-by-step closer to our table. I was mesmerized.

I watched her every move as she got closer and closer to our table. Finally, this tall beauty stopped at our table and with a perfect smile warmly greeted Marc and Tatiana. It was Amanda! Marc was right; Amanda was an incredibly beautiful woman!

She sat down and we were introduced. Of course I wanted to play it cool like any good looking, Lebanese businessman knows how, not letting anyone on to the fact that as for me it was love at first sight. "It's nice to meet you", I said in my deepest baritone voice.

It did not take long before I was amazed at another quality Amanda had apart from being the most beautiful woman on the face of planet earth. Amanda was surprisingly bold! Her speech was truthful, honest, and forthright and at the same time conscientious and caring. She was bold in a pure, good and loving way.

Amanda shared with Marc and Tatiana what Jesus had done in her life and what He could do in theirs unapologetically and with grace. She spoke the truth in love. It was so refreshing and even convicting to be in her presence. She was on fire! Part way through the meal, a couple from another table walked over to the four of us and introduced themselves. They were so impressed by our conversation and God talk that they wanted to participate. I had never seen anything like it. Revival was breaking out at Pierre's Restaurant of South Brunswick, New Jersey!

Often times when we think about sharing our faith we become intimidated. Our mind becomes barraged with an assortment of questions, doubts, fears, and other vices that keep us held back. We become afraid of not knowing what to say, of what people will think of us, and how they will respond. All of these fears create a snare that holds us back from accomplishing God's will for our lives and theirs.

Fear of man will prove to be a snare, but whoever trusts in the LORD is kept safe. (Proverbs 29:25)

If fear is the diagnosis, what then is the cure? Two words can describe it—bold love. We need a large dose of Holy Chutzpah. Amanda had it. The Apostles had it. Jesus of course had it in a major way. He was bold and confident. He was unafraid, unashamed, and unapologetic. He had real, Holy Chutzpah!

Take Jesus' interaction with the Samaritan woman He met by Jacob's well. As the story goes, Jesus was leaving Judea and on His way to Galilee. Now we have all likely heard the mathematical statement that the shortest path between two points is a straight line—pretty simple idea. Walking in a straight line from point A to point B is better than following a curve or taking an unnecessary detour. The shortest distance for Jesus' voyage from Judea to Galilee would be to go through Samaria, a straight shot.

Yet in those days, many pious Jewish people would not take the quick route home. In fact, they would walk miles out of their way just to avoid Samaria. You see within Samaria lived the Samaritans. Now that makes sense. In the eyes of the religious Jews of Jesus' day, a Samaritan was a half breed who had mixed the purity of Judaism with paganism and was therefore considered not only unworthy, but unclean. So instead of taking the short route, these Jews would travel east, cross the Jordan River, and enter into the land of Perea to walk around Samaria and avoid any possible contact with a Samaritan.

Jesus would have been quite familiar with this custom of His day and the pressure would have been on for Him to conform to the idea of avoiding Samaria and taking the longer, but "holier" route through Perea. "But He needed to go through Samaria" (John 4:4 NKJV). Time out; hold the presses. Jesus, we need to have a talk with You. You *needed* to go through Samaria? Let's rewrite the story for you, Lord. The story is supposed to read, "But He needed *to avoid* Samaria, so He went through Perea." That is strike one for Jesus. He should have known to avoid such a place like Samaria. Tisk, Tisk!

But wait, it only gets worse. Jesus is wearied by the long journey and stops by a well for something to drink. Only one problem, Jesus did not bring a bucket. So He did what any of us would do, He asked the person who came to the well if He could get a drink of water. No big deal, right? Wrong. First of all, He not only asked the next person at the well for the drink, He asked the next *female* person at the well. Jesus, this is strike two for You today. If that is not bad enough, this woman was a Samaritan! Time out, once again Jesus; we need to have a talk. Don't You know that what You are doing is taboo?

In fact, not only were the Jews aware of this sacrilegious act of Jesus, so was the Samaritan woman! Finally, someone is going to set this wild and audacious Jesus straight. She says to Jesus, "You are a Jew and I am a Samaritan woman. How can you ask me for a drink?" (For Jews do not associate with Samaritans.)" (John 4:9). It sounds like this lady had her own share of holy chutzpah! She is a bit puzzled by His request for a sip of water and decides to inform Him that this type of thing just is not supposed to happen. Let's contextualize to our own era. This would be like a white man asking a black woman for a drink of water during the days of Jim Crow laws in America.

Jesus was breaking down a big time racial barrier in this moment, one that could have some serious repercussions and critique from His peers.

It didn't faze Him. He goes on to challenge the woman with these words, "If you knew the gift of God and who it is that asks you for a drink, you would have asked him and he would have given you living water" (John 4:10). Jesus was beginning to slide down the sanity scale in this woman's mind from the side of ignorant closer to the far end labeled insane. How can a guy with no bucket promise her living water? It is at this point that I imagine the Samaritan woman speaks to Jesus in a heavily sarcastic tone as she interrogates Him with questions.

"Sir," the woman said, "you have nothing to draw with and the well is deep. Where can you get this living water? Are you greater than our father Jacob, who gave us the well and drank from it himself, as did also his sons and his livestock?" (John 4:12)

Before we continue on in the story, let's take a moment to see how this applies to you and me as we think about sharing our faith with the world around us. We know from reading ahead in the story that Jesus is really out to help this woman more than He is just trying to sponge a drink of water off of her. He is offering her living spiritual water, the hope of new life, and the opportunity to experience wholeness. All He gets in return is disrespect, back talk, and rejection, but it does not deter Him. Why? One simple reason, Jesus had bold love. His love was greater than any fear, pride, and prejudices all combined. His perfect love was not going to lose this battle.

Jesus' love would overcome, not by force or power, but by determination and persistence. Bold love never gives up. Bold love never fears evil. Bold love prevails, even unto death.

There is no fear in love. But perfect love drives out fear, because fear has to do with punishment. The one who fears is not made perfect in love. (1 John 4:18)

If you want to overcome all fear and intimidation of sharing your faith with the people in your sphere of influence and those who come across your path, the solution comes down to this one truth. God's love perfected in you is greater than every other force or power in the world around you, which explains the boldness of Jesus. Jesus was so secure in the Father's love for Him that He could not be intimidated, backed down or patronized. Jesus' love for humanity was grounded in God's love for Him.

**So what is the solution to overcoming fear and doubt
when sharing the good news of Jesus to a lost world?
It is one simple truth. Believe God loves you.**

*For God so loved the world that he gave his one and only Son,
that whoever believes in him shall not perish but have eternal
life.* (John 3:16)

God's love for humanity was the impetus by which God sent Jesus
on a mission to save the world. God's love for us is the same force and
power that motivates us to share the message of Christ to the world.

*For Christ's love compels us, because we are convinced that one
died for all, and therefore all died.* (2 Corinthian 5:14)

Love Does Extravagant Things

People will do extravagant things for love. After I met my wife and
we dated for some time I felt like God wanted me to propose to her. So
I set up a day for us to go out together and eventually end up in a park
that we enjoyed. Under one of the pavilions in the park, I got down on
one knee and proposed to Amanda.

She was speechless and shocked, but she eventually said, "Yes."

As we left the park, we saw a beautiful black limousine parked
right by my car.

I played dumb, "Wow, look at that limo! I wonder what it is
here for."

As we got closer, I invited Amanda to go inside. Our limo driver
escorted us back to Pierre's restaurant, the same place where we had
met on our first blind date. I arranged with Pierre, the owner, to have
a private table in a secluded loft area of the restaurant. We had a wonderful meal and we had plenty of time to gaze into each other's eyes,

and for Amanda to examine her new shiny diamond engagement ring. But the night was not yet over! As we left the restaurant, the limo driver awaited us again. We got inside the vehicle and there sat two of Amanda's best friends and her mother Diane. It was like a mini surprise party in the limousine! We drove around town, enjoyed some champagne, and rejoiced over the new exciting future before us!

God's love did the most extravagant thing of all. His love paid for more than a nice meal at a beautiful restaurant and a limo ride. His love paid for the redemption of the entire world! And that, my friend, is something to get really excited about! God loved us enough that He allowed His only Son Jesus to come down into a world dominated by sin and evil in order to rescue us from Satan's grip and from hell.

The reason the Son of God appeared was to destroy the devil's work. (1 John 3:8)

Jesus' bold love drew Him to Samaria to see the woman at the well and let her know she could find redemption. He explained to her, "Everyone who drinks of this water will thirst again; but whoever drinks of the water that I will give him shall never thirst; but the water that I will give him will become in him a well of water springing up to eternal life" (John 4:13-14). At this point, something Jesus said struck a chord with the woman. She was intrigued, curious, and even thirsty for this living water.

We have once again encountered the ingenious nature of Jesus. Here He is, a man without a bucket, willingly offering this woman a drink of living water. It is an invitation extraordinaire, and it is a lesson for us in making our own invitations to the world around us. We must make the offer irresistible! Jesus calls us to be fishers of men (and woman). While I am no expert in fishing, I do know this one thing. You never cast a line out with only a hook. A good fisherman knows just the right type of bait to lure the fish. So we also must make sure we present the good news of Jesus with bait on the line, not just a hook. In other words, we need to let people know what God offers them through Jesus Christ.

Just consider for a moment all that Jesus offers the person who willingly submits their life into His hands. He provides forgiveness, healing, restoration, peace, a new start on life, a relationship with God, eternal bliss, hope, wisdom, grace, truth, courage, power, strength, and while the list can and will go on for all eternity, it all comes down to this one thing—unconditional, unimaginable, unfathomable, amazing LOVE! The love of Jesus is the most powerful gift in the universe and it is ours to freely offer the world!

Jesus humbled Himself before the Samaritan woman, asking for water, when He was the creator of water—both physical and spiritual. He did not have a bucket, but He did have the power to forgive this woman's sins and the love to redeem her soul.

She expected rejection, He gave her acceptance. She expected judgment; Jesus showed her mercy.

He risked the rejection, accusation, and judgment of His peers and the scorn of His disciples because His love was so great. He loved her enough to bring up the topic of sin in her life, but not until He first embraced her and drew her in by His unconditional love and acceptance. What results did Jesus get from offering the Samaritan woman living water? Let's tune back in and hear her response.

> *The woman said to him, "Sir, give me this water so that I won't get thirsty and have to keep coming here to draw water." (John 4:15)*

She took the bait! Good work, Jesus! Now, just lead her in a simple prayer so she can accept You into her life and follow You and we will move on to the next story. Let's watch how Jesus closes the deal, reels in the fish, and adds a new follower to His nets.

(Jesus) told her, "Go, call your husband and come back."
(John 4:16)

What? Really, Jesus? You already know this woman has lived a pretty loose life. Did You really have to bring up her relational "issues"?

"I have no husband," she replied. (John 4:17a)

Okay, Jesus here is the time to lay on the grace and mercy really thick. Tell her You are sorry she is no longer with her husband, move on to a prayer, and give her a copy of the Old Testament. Let's make sure she accepts You on the spot before she loses interest!

Jesus said to her, "You are right when you say you have no husband. The fact is, you have had five husbands, and the man you now have is not your husband. What you have just said is quite true." (John 4:17a-18)

Now You have done it Jesus. You are highlighting this woman's sins. I do not think she is going to like that very much. Well, let's look on the bright side. There are other fish in the sea you can go after.

"Sir," the woman said, "I can see that you are a prophet. Our ancestors worshiped on this mountain, but you Jews claim that the place where we must worship is in Jerusalem."

"Woman," Jesus replied, "believe me, a time is coming when you will worship the Father neither on this mountain nor in Jerusalem. You Samaritans worship what you do not know; we worship what we do know, for salvation is from the Jews. Yet a time is coming and has now come when the true worshipers will worship the Father in the Spirit and in truth, for they are the kind of worshipers the Father seeks. God is spirit, and his worshipers must worship in the Spirit and in truth."

The woman said, "I know that Messiah (called Christ) is coming. When he comes, he will explain everything to us."

Then Jesus declared, "I, the one speaking to you—I am he." (John 4:19-26)

Amazing, bold, and beautiful—that is the best way to describe Jesus' direct style with this woman. He captivated her with the offer of living water. She took the bait. Then He moved to the hook. He brought light to the areas of darkness in her life—a bold move. If that was not enough, He went further to explain the errors in her religious thinking and presented God to her in spirit and in truth. Finally, when Jesus was sure the hook was firmly planted in the fish's cheeks, He revealed Himself to her as the Messiah. The boldness of Jesus cuts both ways.

Boldness first welcomes everyone with open arms and no judgment. Boldness then speaks to the heart of what really keeps a person from God in their life.

It was not just Holy Chutzpah, it was the Holy Spirit! Being filled with the Holy Spirit and His power is the only way we too can grow to be like Jesus in our boldness of faith, love and demonstration of miracles, signs, and wonders. Jesus spoke to the disciples some final words before He went back to heaven.

"But you will receive power when the Holy Spirit comes on you; and you will be my witnesses in Jerusalem, and in all Judea and Samaria, and to the ends of the earth." (Acts 1:8)

What an amazing promise! God promises to give us power to be His witnesses to the entire world. The word power in our English Bible comes from the Greek word *dunamis* (doo'-nam-is) in the original manuscript. It is a word that means force, miraculous power, ability, abundance, strength, and mighty work.[4] The Apostle Paul describes this power in our lives this way, "His incomparably great power for us who believe. That power is the same as the mighty strength he exerted when he raised Christ from the dead and seated him at his right hand in the heavenly realms" (Ephesians 1:20).

The power within us through the Holy Spirit is the same power that raised Jesus Christ from the dead! Now that is some dynamic power! Paul again emphasizes the work of this power within our lives when he states that God is "able to do immeasurably more than all we ask or imagine, according to his power that is at work within us" (Ephesians 3:20).

So what is the key to Growing Out in our expression of who Jesus is to the world? It is simply this: we are to live out God's bold love in the power of the Holy Spirit. It was the way of Jesus and the way of the early disciples. Jesus taught that His miracles were the proof that His words were true and He was one with the Father (John 10:25, 37-38, 14:11). Peter and John did not have silver or gold, but they had the power of Jesus inside them to heal the lame man and make him walk (Acts 3:6). Paul did not have wise and persuasive words, but he had a demonstration of the Spirit's power (1 Corinthians 2:4).

If you desire to be effective in your work for Jesus and Grow Out to reach more people, you do not need a formula. You do not need a system. You do not need a program. Formulas, systems, and programs all have their place and serve their purposes, but they can never substitute for the real work of God. To see God work through us to reach people for Jesus, we must ask God for His love and His power!

---

[4] *Strong's Greek Dictionary* 1411

Remember These Truths and Take Action

- If fear is the diagnosis, bold love is the cure.
- Jesus' love overcomes, not by force or power, but by determination and persistence. Bold love never gives up. Bold love never fears evil. Bold love prevails, even unto death.
- The solution to overcoming fear and doubt when sharing the good news of Jesus starts by believing God loves you.
- A good fisherman knows just the right type of bait to lure the fish. In the same way, we must make sure we present the good news of Jesus with bait on the line, not just a hook. In other words, we need to let people know what God offers them through Jesus Christ.
- We are to live out God's bold love in the power of the Holy Spirit.

Personal Reflection and Group Discussion Questions

- What makes talking to others about Jesus intimidating?
- Jesus had to overcome many barriers to reach the Samaritan woman. What type of barriers exist when you seek to share your faith with others?
- How would you define the term "bold love"?
- What good things about knowing God are important to share with people who do not know Him?

Meditation

God's bold love for me and within me is greater than all my fears.

Prayer

God, empower me with bold love through Your Holy Spirit.

Bible References

- Proverbs 29:25
- John 4:1-26
- John 3:16
- 2 Corinthians 5:14
- 1 John 3:8
- Acts 1:8
- Ephesians 1:20
- Ephesians 3:20
- John 10:25, 37-38, 14:11
- Acts 3:6
- 1 Corinthians 2:4

Chapter 8

God's Nutrition Plan

I started to lift weights at an early age, probably around twelve. My brother Paul was an active bodybuilder who opened his own gym where I would work out. Paul taught me how to use the equipment and have proper form as well as the importance of proper diet and exercise. As I grew older into my teens, I followed in my brother's footsteps and took up bodybuilding myself. I even competed in a couple teenage bodybuilding contests. Fortunately, I was encouraged by my brother Paul to take the natural route to health and avoid steroids or other illegal performance enhancing substances.

By my junior year of college, I had grown considerably in size and strength. I started to work out with the football players in the weight room and decided to try out for the team my senior year. The football season always began before the school year, so I had to go back early to school, live in a dorm setting with the other players, and enjoy the grueling twice a day practice schedule.

My roommate during pre-season football camp was a guy who had played football all his life and was a bit on the wild side. I think squirrely might be a better word to describe him. He was truly without fear or reservation when it came to playing football. When it came to life, he was a bit reckless as well. I remember him looking at all my vitamins, supplements, and protein powders stacked up on a shelf in our small two single bed dorm room and saying to me, "You would be better off just taking steroids. It would be a lot cheaper, easier, and more effective." That was the route he had taken and he was not ashamed to admit it.

Our spiritual lives are much like our physical bodies. If we exercise and feed ourselves with good, healthy food and drink, we will grow to be strong and healthy. If we feast on fried and sugary food, we will not only feel lethargic and slow, we will end up looking more like a football than a football player. Just like there are illegal substances that promise a quicker return on our investment, there are also counterfeit spiritual solutions that falsely promise to help us grow quicker and stronger without any real work and no consequences.

Growing deeper with God is a journey that requires us to eat and drink spiritually healthy food and water, but also to exercise our faith in a way that promotes our spiritual growth.

A balanced diet of God's Word and the refreshing waters of the Holy Spirit will not only make us stronger, they will draw us closer to the one who made us.

My brother not only taught me how to eat properly and to exercise, he also taught me the importance of discipline. Eating right for one day is not enough to build a strong body. Exercising sporadically never developed a champion in any sport. It takes regular, consistent training to grow and develop.

I was backstage at a bodybuilding contest many years ago talking with one of the competitors who was in no shape to be wearing a Speedo® in front of strangers. Somehow this guy was oblivious to the fact that he was not in the right shape to be competing. He boasted to me, "I've been dieting for a whole week!" He did not understand that the other competitors had spent months dieting and working to sculpt and train their bodies into shape.

Spiritually speaking, it is important to develop the daily discipline of eating the right foods and drinking the right drink in order to build a strong, growing, and healthy relationship with God. One day or one week of devotionals is good, but it is the consistent working out of prayer, Bible study and time with God over years that truly develops us into spiritually fit men and woman of God.

> *Train yourself to be godly. For physical training is of some value, but godliness has value for all things, holding promise for both the present life and the life to come. (1 Timothy 4:7b-8)*

Jesus began His ministry with a fast from all food and drink. He was sent to the wilderness by the Holy Spirit to spend time alone with and draw closer to His heavenly Father. It was a spiritual huddle with the Father where Jesus would tune into heaven's frequency and listen to His Father's directives for the mission that awaited Him.

Like any good heroic story, we always have a villain who tries to trump the plans of the hero. After reaching the fortieth day of His fast, Jesus was hungry, weak and vulnerable. We should not be surprised to find that at just the same time Satan showed up to run a play of interference against the offensive strategy of God and His quarterback Jesus.

> *Be alert and of sober mind. Your enemy the devil prowls around like a roaring lion looking for someone to devour. (1 Peter 5:8)*

Satan's mission was to cause Jesus to doubt and deny the plays God was calling from heaven, and for Jesus to worship him instead of God. His plan is the same for each of our own lives. It is to distract us, deceive us, and defeat us.

> *The tempter came to him and said, "If you are the Son of God, tell these stones to become bread." (Matthew 4:3)*

Notice two things. First of all, Satan goes after Jesus' identity before he tempts Him to sin. "If you are the Son of God..." Now why would he do such a thing? The answer is simple. We all live out of our identity—who we think we are and what we believe about ourselves.

Our actions are only a bi-product of our belief system about God, ourselves, and the world around us.

If Satan can get us to believe we are unworthy, hopeless or abandoned, we will start to live as if we truly are. Then we will end up making choices that align with this false identity instead of our true identity as defined by God in Christ.

Notice Satan's second enticement, "Tell these stones to become bread." Satan is always offering the short cut, the deviation, the quick and dirty path in life. He wants to offer you steroids instead of telling you to exercise and eat your veggies. "Do a miracle, Jesus. Quit this silly little fast and eat some bread. You know you are hungry. Just use your power to please yourself." What a snake! Now pay attention to the response of Jesus.

Jesus answered, "It is written: 'Man shall not live on bread alone, but on every word that comes from the mouth of God.'" (Matthew 4:3-4)

So much for Satan's ploy! Jesus was not tricked by the vain appeal to the quick and cheap route to success. Instead, He chose to stick with God's plan as found in His Word.

Do you enjoy fresh baked bread? Now I know all the bad things they say about bread these days, especially white bread. Even if you are allergic to gluten or are on a low carb diet, you just cannot deny that fresh baked bread is delicious. Even the smell of it is enough to make your mouth water. If you go to a restaurant and they bring out fresh, hot bread it is like a gift from heaven, especially if they give you some tasty olive oil or seasoned butter for dipping. I am making myself hungry!

In my opinion, bread truly is a gift of God. I mean after all, if bread was not Jesus' favorite food, then why would Satan tempt Him with it on His fast? He could have offered Jesus fried worms, chocolate covered ants or even a piña colada but he knew that would not have enticed Jesus. Instead he offered Jesus bread. It is my guess that Satan knew Jesus was a fan of bread.

The significance of bread in Bible times was more than a measure of flour and dough. It had spiritual meaning. "As the mainstay of life, bread came to be a primary metaphor for life and sustenance."[5] Knowing the importance of bread, it was no accident that Jesus chose to call Himself the "Bread of Life" (John 6:35). By this title, Jesus was proclaiming He was the source of true spiritual life and vitality.

Jesus spoke the Word of God to refute Satan's lies stating that people do not live by physical bread alone; rather, we need the life giving bread of God's Word to sustain us. Without God's Word a person can have a pulse, but not truly be alive. It is the Word of God that sustains us and makes us strong and prosperous. The Greek word for "word" in this text is *rhema* (hray'-mah). *Rhema* is the spoken word of God. *Rhema* is a timely word that hits home to your heart. "A person finds joy in giving an apt reply— and how good is a timely word!" (Proverbs 15:23). *Logos* (log'-os) is God's Word in its entirety whereas *rhema* is God's Word for the moment.

Imagine looking through a phone book. Do you remember those things? (For all my young readers, a phone book was a physical book you would use to look up someone's phone number before you had the Internet or cell phones. It also served as a booster seat for kids at the dinner table.) The phone book represents *logos*. It has everyone's phone number in it. *Rhema* would be when you found the number you were looking for in the book. "Oh, there is Mrs. Jone's number."

Two-Way Communication with God

Jesus is informing us that to truly live a life *for* God and more importantly a life *with* God, we must be able to hear *from* God.

---

5 Elwell, Walter A. "Entry for 'Bread, Bread of Presence'". "Evangelical Dictionary of Theology". 1997.

We must be able to receive God's message, hear His voice, discern His will, and understand His calling. We must have two-way communication with God. I am totally serious about this. God wants to communicate with you and have an on-going conversation and relationship. That is what Jesus had and that is what God wants for you, too. To be like Jesus in every way means to have a direct line to God the Father where He communicates to you and you communicate back to Him.

Jesus said that He did nothing in life unless He first heard from God. (John 5:19). Jesus learned to live by every word God spoke. In the same way, Jesus promised that we would be able to hear His voice. "My sheep listen to my voice; I know them and they follow me." (John 10:27). Hearing from God is not a right reserved for full-time clergy. Instead it is the privilege and right of every believer in Jesus. We can all hear God because we all have the Holy Spirit living within us speaking to our heart, mind and soul.

So when it comes to hearing from God, what are the ground rules? The first rule is go to God's Word, the Bible. It is a common request for God loving people to want to know God's will for their lives.

If you want God's will, you must read God's Word.

God's Word, the Bible, is a precious gift to mankind. It is a light that shines before us to give us the path to follow (Psalm 119:105). The better you know God's Word, the *logos*, the easier it will be to discern God's voice and His will for your life (Romans 12:1-2). God's written Word is the first place to go when you want to hear from God. It is written in black and white for us. We just need to sit at the table and eat of it. The more we eat God's Word, the more we desire it. The more we desire it, the more it comes alive. The more it comes alive, the more we come alive in our relationship with God and in every other area of life. God's Word is bread that gives life!

God's Word is the first source of input He wants to put in our brains and hearts to know Him better. But more than a telephone book of information, God wants to give you revelation. That is where the Holy Spirit comes into play. God's Spirit living within us gives us the ability to hear from God directly. It is like God has given you His own personal phone number. God still speaks and He wants you to pick up the phone and listen. Instead of listening with our ears for an audible, external voice, God has now internalized His voice so we just have to listen from within. Now do not get me wrong. I am not suggesting we try and listen for our inner self or conscience. I am saying we need to become acutely aware of the voice of the Holy Spirit living within us.

Over the years as I have grown closer to God, the greatest means of knowing God's will apart from the Bible has been listening to His "still, small, voice" speak to my heart. If that term is new to you, let me explain what it means in a practical way that will help you make sense of this idea. Throughout your day, you are bombarded with messages.

"Don't forget to pick up the kids after their practice."

"The report is due on Monday morning."

"Buy flowers for your wife tonight on your way home."

"Don't forget to take the dog for his shots."

"You are no good, unworthy, and have failed and disappointed God."

Some of the messages we hear running in our head come from our brain running through the list of ideas, to do items, and thoughts. It is a natural and amazing phenomenon of being a human being. Other ideas and thoughts that seem to jump into our head are sent by Satan and his demonic forces to distract, discourage, and deceive us. Then, there are God thoughts or impressions to lift us higher, take us deeper, and guide us to the path by which we hear and know God's will.

Every morning I take time to journal in prayer with God. I sit in a quiet room with no interference from the dog, the kids, my wife, the television or any other outside stimuli (except maybe a warm cup of coffee). In these times alone with God, I will ask Him an open ended question like, "How do You want to encourage me today?" Or "What one truth do You want me to keep in mind as I go about my day?" After writing out my questions, I pause, quiet myself, and listen.

I am not listening for a booming voice or a thunderous clap from heaven. Instead, I am listening to the rhythm of my heart. I am listening to the soft messages that are being impressed upon my mind and my spirit.

Mark Virkler in describing the voice of God within us says, "God's voice in your heart often sounds like a flow of spontaneous thoughts."[6]

"You are a good son. I am pleased with what you are doing. Keep up the good work. I am 100 percent behind you."

As I hear these impressions, I write them down (actually I type them on my computer) and sit still to process the words I have received.

Do they line up with God's Word?

Do they line up with God's character?

Are they edifying, encouraging, uplifting, refining, convicting, but not condemning?

Do they bring life?

Do they bring me closer to the light of God or further into the darkness of sin and selfishness?

Do they cause me to love God, others, and myself in a healthy way or are they accusatory and condemning?

As I contemplate the words put on my heart, I allow them to sink down into my soul. God's Word to us is food to our spirit. Whether in the written form of the Bible or the soft spoken words He gives us in prayer, His word truly is the Bread of Life. We all need it to live,

---

[6] *4 Keys to Hearing God–You Can Hear God's Voice!* http://www.cwgministries.org/ Four-Keys-to-Hearing-Gods-Voice, accessed September 5, 2014.

to move, and to have our being found perfectly centered in the living words of Christ. When was the last time you got alone and quieted yourself to hear from God through His Word and in prayer?

Moldy Bread

The other day my son went to make a sandwich for himself. He brought out the scrumptious sub rolls that my wife had purchased from the supermarket just a day or two prior. He looked at the roll and saw a small black spot that he thought was a bruise. Wait a second, son! Bread does not bruise. Let me take a look at that bread. Guess what I found? Yes, you are right. It was covered with mold. It infected the whole loaf. Guess what we did with the loaf. You are right; we threw it out!

In this world there are many types of moldy bread that you just need to throw in the garbage bag. You can eat it, but it will make you sick. It might taste good going down, but it will not leave you healthy and strong. You may end up throwing it back up or seeing it run ugly through your life in liquid form. Bad bread in the spiritual sense comes from all the lies we believe as well as the false voices that come from the occult or other satanic sources.

Satan wants for us to believe his lies about ourselves, lies about God and lies about others. "When [Satan] lies, he speaks his native language, for he is a liar and the father of lies" (John 8:44c). He is crafty enough to speak these lies in the first person to our hearts. If you are a child of God today, you must know that believing thoughts like, "I am no good" or "I am worthless" or "I am hopeless" is like smoking a full pack of Satan's lies; it is lethal. The way we defeat these lies is by believing the truth of who we are in Christ. "I am redeemed." "I am forgiven." "I am accepted and loved by God."

Satan attempts to distance us from our Lord by lying to us about God's true nature and being. "God has abandoned me." "God does not love me." "God is upset with me." Satan wants us to believe we are condemned by God, but the truth is that we are no longer condemned because of Christ's death on the cross for our sins (Romans 8:1, 1 John 3:20, 21). Speaking the truth of God's love and promises over your life will defeat Satan's lies. "God loves me." "God accepts me." "God has forgiven me completely."

If Satan is not lying to us about ourselves or God, he is lying about other people. He brings false accusation against our fellow brothers and sisters in Christ to discredit their testimony, shame God's name and cause division among God's people (Revelation 12:10). Do not fall for Satan's lies! Dialogue openly with others avoiding gossip and judging at all costs. If you diligently seek to walk in love and forgiveness towards others you will surely suffocate Satan's destructive lies in your relationships.

Another way Satan deploys lies into our lives is through occult practices. Some people think that reading the horoscope or playing the Ouija board or going to palm readers is just a form of fun and entertainment. Others will even ascribe great power and authority to these sources of input. Friend, from me to you, let me tell you the truth, this stuff is not just moldy old bread, it is spiritual poison of the worst kind! Better than me telling you, take it directly from God's Word.

> *When someone tells you to consult mediums and spiritists, who whisper and mutter, should not a people inquire of their God? Why consult the dead on behalf of the living? Consult God's instruction and the testimony of warning. If anyone does not speak according to this word, they have no light of dawn.* (Isaiah 8:19-20)

> *Let no one be found among you who sacrifices their son or daughter in the fire, who practices divination or sorcery, interprets omens, engages in witchcraft, or casts spells, or who is a medium or spiritist or who consults the dead. Anyone who does these things is detestable to the Lord; because of these same detestable practices the Lord your God will drive out those nations before you.* (Deuteronomy 18:10-12)

If you are currently engaged in any of these occult activities, I have some simple advice for you. Leave that moldy bread alone! It will inevitably make you sick and alienate you from the one true God. Jesus is the true "bread of life." So, why settle for any counterfeits?

A Life Yielded to the Holy Spirit

If you truly want to be spiritual and have a meaningful connection with God, then invite the Holy Spirit to take over and lead your life. The Holy Spirit is the most genuine, real, and authentic form of spiritual vitality one can find on this earth. You cannot get any higher spiritually than to be immersed with and led by the Holy Spirit.

In reference to the Holy Spirit, Jesus said, "Let anyone who is thirsty come to me and drink. Whoever believes in me, as Scripture has said, rivers of living water will flow from within them" (John 7:37b-38). Rivers of living water, now that sounds refreshing! The promise of Jesus is to provide us with life through the precious gift of the Holy Spirit. If you desire to Grow Deeper in your relationship with God, it is an imperative to become increasingly acquainted with the Holy Spirit in your life.

Some people shy away when you start talking about the Holy Spirit. I think they get afraid of what they cannot control or of what they have seen in other people that comes across as weird, wild or wacky. "But the fruit of the Spirit is love, joy, peace, patience, kindness, goodness, faithfulness, gentleness and self-control. Against such things there is no law" (Galatians 5:22-23 ESV). In other words, the way you truly know if the Holy Spirit is in operation is by the fruit, or the bi-product of a person's lifestyle. I have been blessed to have many encounters and experiences with the Holy Spirit that have brought great joy, laughter, great peace even in the midst of chaos and great patience when I was on fringe of losing my own last wits.

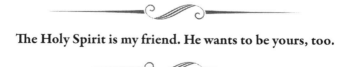

The Holy Spirit is my friend. He wants to be yours, too.

The friendship He offers is more intimate than any human relationship can provide because He chooses to live within us, for life. He inhabits our being, our soul, and even our body.

Don't you know that you yourselves are God's temple and that God's Spirit dwells in your midst? (1 Corinthians 3:16)

God's Word is our food; the Holy Spirit is our drink. He comes to refresh us, to change us, and to empower us to live fully for Jesus. He is our source of power and spiritual strength (Zechariah 4:6). He is the voice within us that guides us to the path God wants us to take. He is also the voice within us that warns us of imminent danger and trouble. He is God and He lives within every person who has given their life to Christ and confessed Him as Lord (Romans 8:9, 1 Corinthians 12:3).

So how does one begin to draw closer to the Holy Spirit? It happens in the same way a person comes to know Christ, by invitation. Just as God invited us to accept Christ as our Savior, He invites us to ask the Holy Spirit to work deeper in our lives and take further control. Control is really what He is looking for, but He is not going to take it by hostile means. He is looking for us to surrender our rights to Him.

When I was a pipsqueak little boy I used to enjoy picking fights with my older brothers. Of course they were bigger, stronger, and a lot heavier than I was at the time, but I had watched enough WWF wrestling to think I had a shot at taking them down. Inevitably, I would end up on the carpet of my family's living room with my cheek to the ground and my brother securely placed over me.

"Say Uncle," he demanded.

I hated to relent and give in to his demands, but I hated rug burn even more, "Uncle! Uncle! Uncle!"

The Holy Spirit does not *typically* work this way. I need to say typically because there are indeed times when He is more forceful to get His way in our lives. If He feels it necessary, He will knock us off our spiritual high horse to get our attention (Acts 9:4). But for the most part, He does not force us into submission with our face to the carpets. Most often He prods us gently and persistently until we choose

His ways and surrender our rights to Him. Each of us has the right to accept and welcome the Spirit's presence and control in our lives or to resist, restrict or even deny Him from having full access.

Do not be afraid of the Holy Spirit. Releasing your control to Him is the wisest and most exhilarating decision you could make in life.

Holy Spirit is gentle, yet strong. He is pure and refreshing like clean water. He comes to bring the life of God deep down within to your very soul. Welcome the Holy Spirit into every aspect of your life and watch to see how He will begin to transform you from the inside out.

Come, all you who are thirsty, come to the waters; and you who have no money, come, buy and eat! Come, buy wine and milk without money and without cost. Why spend money on what is not bread, and your labor on what does not satisfy? Listen, listen to me, and eat what is good, and you will delight in the richest of fare. (Isaiah 55:1-2)

If your desire is to Grow Deeper with God in a close relationship with Him, you must eat the right foods and drink of His living water. As you practice the daily habit of chewing on God's Word, listening to God's voice, and surrendering to the Holy Spirit, your life will steadily grow stronger and your relationship with God will grow deeper over time.

Remember These Truths and Take Action

- If your desire is to Grow Deeper with God in a close relationship with Him, you must eat the right foods and drink of His living water.

- To truly live a life for God and more importantly a life *with* God, we must be able to hear *from* God. God thoughts or impressions lift us higher, take us deeper, and guide us to the path by which we hear and know God's will.

- Do not settle for old, moldy, stale bread. Believing the truth of what God's word says about you, about God and about others will keep you free from Satan's lies. Stay clear from all occult activity.

- If you desire to Grow Deeper in your relationship with God, it is an imperative to become increasingly acquainted with the Holy Spirit in your life.

- Just as God invited us to accept Christ as our Savior, He invites us to ask the Holy Spirit to work deeper in our lives and take further control. Control is really what the Holy Spirit is looking for, but He is not going to take it by hostile means. He is looking for us to surrender our rights to Him.

Personal Reflection and Group Discussion Questions

- Describe the most delicious bread you have tasted? What types of feelings does it provoke?

- Who do you know who takes good care of their physical body? What habits do they practice?

- If you were to get into the best "spiritual shape" as possible, what type of things would you need to include in your diet? What would you need to eliminate or reduce?

- Can you think of a time when you truly knew you heard from God? If so, what was that experience like?

- As an exercise, take a few moments alone with God in a quiet place. Write down one of the following questions, and then listen to the flowing steam of words that come to mind. Write those words down by faith:

God, what words of encouragement do you have for me?

God, how can I have a closer relationship with you?

Meditation

God's Word feeds me. His Spirit refreshes my soul.

Prayer

God, I open my heart to receive Your words and I give the Holy Spirit control of my life.

Bible References

- 1 Timothy 4:7-8
- 1 Peter 5:8
- Matthew 4:3-4
- John 6:35
- Proverbs 15:23
- John 5:19
- John 10:27
- Psalm 119:105
- Romans 12:1-2
- 1 John 3:20, 21
- Revelation 12:10
- John 8:44
- Isaiah 8:19-20
- Deuteronomy 18:10-12
- John 7:37b-38
- Galatians 5:22-23
- 1 Corinthians 3:16
- Zechariah 4:6
- Romans 8:9
- 1 Corinthians 12:3

- Acts 9:4
- Isaiah 55:1-2

Chapter 9

One with God

It was Rich's first day as a consultant on the job. He was joining a team of project managers that I was part of and moved into the cubicle next to me. He became my cube neighbor. Like two grown men with adjacent lockers in high school, we were going to be spending a lot of time rubbing elbows. Rich and I went downstairs to the cafeteria and had lunch together his first day of work. Rich was a conversationalist. (That is a kind way to say he liked to talk a lot.) Not only did he like to talk, I sensed from the start that he was open to talk about basically any topic—how fun.

Sensing Rich would be open to talk about spiritual things, I waited for a good moment in the conversation to bring up my own personal testimony of how God had come into my life. The door seemed to open naturally or maybe better stated supernaturally, and I began to share how God had saved me and dramatically changed my life for the good.

Rich quietly and attentively listened to me without any interruption. He did not cross his arms or show any other signs that he was closed off, bored or angered. So I took my time and shared what God had done in my life and how I came to know God personally. After I was done sharing, Rich told me about a relative of his who had also "become one with the Lord." The expression "become one with the Lord" was not one I used in my testimony, but one that Rich had obviously heard and felt comfortable with as a means to describe a personal conversion to God. At the time, his words struck and ministered back to me. "One with the Lord"—what a great way to describe the intimate nature of a personal relationship with God in Christ!

Relationships with people can take on so many levels. We have people we know about, but have never met, like celebrities or people of antiquity. We have people who we meet once and never meet again, strangers in passing. We have acquaintances, people we know, but are not close to on any level. We have friends, those we confide in and whose company we enjoy. We have close friends and we even have best friends. God desires us to Grow Together with fellow members of His family so relationships are extremely important in God's economy.

Becoming One with the Lord

Along the same lines, a variety of depths exist in a person's relationship with God. You may or may not know God personally today. Maybe you have heard a lot *about* God, but you have never had an encounter *with* God. You may have met God once at a church or a crusade or at a desperate time in your life, but it was for the most part a onetime event. You may be an acquaintance of God's where you talk to Him from time to time, but not with great frequency or depth. Maybe you know God quite well. You talk with Him frequently and even when you are not talking, you are listening or simply resting in His presence regardless of the activity you are involved in.

On the far end of this continuum is the place of becoming "one with the Lord." It is a place that is foreign to many of us. It may be like a tropical island that you visited at one time in your life. "I've been there" and as the t-shirt reads, "Done that." But it is not the place where you stayed to live or are today. Your oneness has waned. Quite possibly it is a place you have never been and even one that you are a bit hesitant to journey toward. After all, what does becoming one with God look like and how will it change the person you are today?

It is God's great desire for all of us to Grow Deeper in our relationship with Him to a place of oneness and intimacy.

Before we go there, let me explain something. In one sense, once you become a child of God, you cannot get any closer to the Lord. I know that seems like a contradiction. In one breathe I am telling you of a place of intimacy and oneness with God that He desires all of us to reach. On the other hand I am suggesting that we cannot get any closer than the day we first met Him. Can both of these axioms be true?

Jesus' death on the cross opened the door for every one of us to enter into a relationship with God. For those of us who choose to turn from our sins and turn to Jesus, we receive the gift of eternal life and also a relationship with God that puts us on His side. We are His. He is ours. Nothing can separate us from the love of God that is in Christ Jesus our Lord (Romans 8:39). So in one sense, we are connected to God and part of His family, in a position of oneness with Him.

Every child born of a mother and father inherit the genes and blood of their biological parents. Similarly, we are all connected to the Father through the blood of His son, Jesus Christ. You are one with God by the death, burial, and resurrection of Jesus that has closed the gap of distance between you and God created by sin. You are now one with God, part of His family. Trying to do good things to please God will not make you more or less part of His family. We are part of His family by the faith we demonstrate in Jesus, not by the things we do (Ephesians 2:8-9, Titus 3:5).

Becoming Team Players

God created marriage to be the most intimate of all family relationships. "That is why a man leaves his father and mother and is united to his wife, and they become one flesh" (Genesis 2:24). When a husband and wife stand side by side and vow to wed the other, they are united and made one together. In essence, they have committed to become one entity instead of two and to walk together as they move forward with their lives.

Yet, if the truth be told, not every couple that has been made one together in holy matrimony shares the unique and holy oneness that God desires. Unfortunately, it is rare in our day. Legally and even spiritually married couples are joined together and are one in the sight of God and the governing authorities of our land. At the same time, relationally and emotionally, there can be distance, a lack of oneness or worse yet, division. Amos 3:3 asks us, "Can two people walk together without agreeing on the direction?" (NLT).

In other words, a couple can by definition be one together, but by practice and lifestyle not walking on a common level of unity and agreement. Picture in your mind's eye two sets of hands being held next to one another in a dark room. A light is on the two sets of hands creating two separate images on the wall. The two sets of hands are the hands of a man and woman who are married. They both have rings on them symbolizing their covenant together. Now imagine with me that the two hands are joined together locking fingers, his then hers, his then hers. Now the image on the wall shows not two sets of hands, but one that is united together. Some couples wear wedding rings, but lack marital intimacy (two images on the wall) while others are united not just in covenant, but in such a way that makes them seem as one unit together.

A football team has many players. On game day the players wear the same color jersey indicating they are part of the same team. Yet, each player has his own unique number expressing his individuality and making him identifiable by the refs, the coaches, and the fans. It is all one team made of many players. In the world of sports, it is not uncommon to hear of professional teams where egos and attitudes rise up to create divisions among teammates. The team still wears the same jersey, they are considered one team by the referees, but there is division among the players that keeps them from functioning like one united force together.

A band that plays music together sounds best when everyone plays the same cord. Multiple soloists strumming to their own beat will create a sound that is hard for the ears to handle. Unity and oneness are "instrumental" in making any family, marriage, team or band work harmoniously.

Now let's take these analogies back to your relationship with God. The day you prayed to God asking Him to forgive your sins and inviting Jesus to be your Savior, you entered into a covenant with Him similar to a marriage covenant between a man and a woman. You may not have understood it to be a covenant, but that is exactly what it was in God's mind. You became wed to God. You became part of His team. You changed alliances and now you are a friend of God instead of being His opponent, or as the Bible states, His enemy (Romans 5:10).

To make things clear, let's be sure we know that everyone who accepts Christ is loved by God and is on His team. We are all His children. We all have the same jersey that reads, "God's Kids" on it. We are in His family, and He loves us and accepts us (Ephesians 1:6). The question is not whether or not we are saved, loved or accepted by God. That has been settled.

> *This is how God showed His love among us: He sent His one and only Son into the world that we might live through Him.* (1 John 4:9)

At this point, we are not talking about our allegiance to God, but our closeness to Him. We are not questioning if we are His children, but if we are His close friends. It is not a question of whether we are wed to God and in covenant with Him—although that is a fair question for all of us to ask.

> *Examine yourselves to see whether you are in the faith; test yourselves. Do you not realize that Christ Jesus is in you—unless, of course, you fail the test?* (2 Corinthians 13:5)

Once you have passed the test by examining yourself as to whether you truly believe Jesus is the Son of God, and have turned from your sins and placed your faith in His saving grace, you move on to another, deeper question.

Are you *one with God* or are you just on the same team together?

Do you just share the same jersey or are you standing side by side in unity with Him?

The great news of the Gospel is that God has made a way for each of us to draw closer to Him. Here is the promise God makes to every one of His children. "Come near to God and He will come near to you" (James 4:8a). Herein lays an amazing promise that we need to unpack.

God has offered us an opportunity, an open door if you will, for all people to draw near to Him from the heart and to know Him intimately. Truly, He has placed no limitations on how close we can get or how far we can go with Him.

Drawing Close to God

Before you take this for granted and say to yourself, "Of course, a benevolent and loving God would want us to be close to Him," you need to understand a few things.

Drawing close to God in this intimate way was not always easy. Before Jesus died for our sins, getting *really* close to God was still possible, but it was more challenging and limited. In God's former covenant with humanity (found in the Old Testament), only the High Priest would be able to enter God's temple into a place called the Holy of Holies. By its name, you can figure out that this was the holiest of all places, one in which the High Priest could truly experience God's presence.

My family lives in a small ranch home in a suburban town of Pennsylvania. We have a bay window that opens up to our kitchen. The beauty of this bay window is that it provides a lot of light into our house. The downside is that any passerby can simply walk by and look right into our household and see our family dynamics. "Is that Tony Capito on their Wheaties box?" In fact, without any obstructions, they can probably see through our house from the window in the front to the one in the back!

At nighttime, however, we have a ritual where we close the curtains and shut out the world from all activity going on inside our dwelling place. (Note to Paparazzi: Come before 9:30 pm on week nights.) When the curtains are shut, only those who are inside the house can see what takes place. Things happen behind the curtains that are private, limited, and even may I dare suggest sacred. For all you know, I could be dancing on the kitchen table to Footloose in my undies!

The High Priest held the highest possible position of all leaders of Israel. He was like the CEO to an organization, the chief of a tribe or better yet like the Pope to the Roman Catholic Church. He was at the top of the food chain. Nobody was in a higher place of authority, accountability or intimacy with God than this one man. He was the sole person who was given the rights by God to visit Him behind the curtains.

Once a year, the High Priest would enter into this sacred place by passing through a curtain separating this unique and sacred area of the temple. At this time, the High Priest would come offering sacrifices for the forgiveness of his sins and the sins of all God's people (Hebrews 9:7). The stakes were high and God took this sacred moment seriously.

"Before the high priest entered the Holy of Holies on the Day of Atonement, he had to wash himself, put on special clothing, bring burning incense to let the smoke cover his eyes from a direct view of God, and bring sacrificial blood with him to make atonement for sins."[7] So much for the notion of waltzing into God's presence nonchalantly!

Jesus' death on the cross for our sins changed this routine and practice dramatically. Among His many titles, Jesus is known in God's new covenant (found in the New Testament) as the Great High Priest

---

[7] "What was the Holy of Holies?" http://www.gotquestions.org/Holy-of-Holies. html, accessed September 5, 2014

(Hebrews 4:14). As the High Priest for all humanity, Jesus gave His own body as the ultimate sacrifice before God. When He did, the literal and spiritual veil that separated common man from the holiness of God was torn in two from top to bottom (Mark 15:28).

The implications of this divine act of God are profound. No longer is the presence of God limited to one man and spiritual authority such as the High Priest (or the Pope, Bishops, Priests, Pastors, Ministers, or any other clergyman or woman for that matter). Nor do we need to go through another human being to get access to God; it is open to all of mankind. "For there is one God and one mediator between God and mankind, the man Christ Jesus, who gave Himself as a ransom for all people" (1 Timothy 2:5-6a).

Now with the curtain torn in two, even the vilest of sinners can come to know God personally and even intimately. "Therefore (Jesus) is able to save completely those who come to God through Him, because He always lives to intercede for them" (Hebrews 7:25). The drug pusher can become an intimate friend of God as well as the prostitute, pimp, and charlatan. Jesus has removed **all** limitations in order to allow **all** people the privilege of drawing near to God! When God says **all**, He means **all**!

Admittedly, it is tempting to just include the first half of the verse, "Come near to God and He will come near to you." That sounds nice, sweet, and open ended. It is like a neon open sign on the front door of a restaurant, "We Are Open." Or as a church sign near my house reads, "All are welcome. We mean it." It is true. This is God's invitation for **all** people who will make Jesus their Lord to draw near to God. His curtains are wide open! The promise is simple. If we draw near to God, He in return will draw near to us, done deal.

Before we draw close to meet with God, we need to read the fine print of the second half of the verse. "Wash your hands, you sinners, and purify your hearts, you double-minded" (James 4:8b). Now that is not a verse you will find being sold as a plaque at your local Christian bookstore! God does welcome us with open arms into His presence. However, the door to God's house has a welcome mat out front and we are expected to take off our dirty shoes before we enter His home.

The desire to draw closer is done on God's terms, not ours. God opens the door of His home for us to be behind the curtain when we first turn from our sins and turn to God for redemption. The distance that sin creates between us and God has been taken care of in the ultimate, eternal, and positional sense by Jesus Christ. We cannot add to His work on the cross one iota and neither should we even try. This is not about developing our own form of right standing with God. That is a worthless pursuit of religiosity that will get you to the land of the frustrated and burn out really quickly. It is a matter of finding our right standing with God by faith in Jesus.

Every person in a family is related by birth or by adoption. However, not every family member has the same level of closeness with their other siblings, Mom or Dad. In God's family, there are children who are close kin to God and then there are children who are far away, like the prodigal son. The door of close relationship is open to everyone in the family through Jesus' shed blood, but the requirements of a close friendship with God are a repentant and remorseful heart. "The sacrifice you desire is a broken spirit. You will not reject a broken and repentant heart, O God" (Psalm 51:17 NLT). We need to approach God in humility recognizing our unworthiness.

At the same time, we need to approach God with great boldness. Now that is an interesting combination—humility and boldness. How does that work? In one sense, we realize that we are sinners who have no right and privilege to stand before a holy God. His curtains are shut to those who have sinned. We are not allowed inside to meet Him. Then Jesus comes on the scene and willingly pours out His blood as the ultimate sacrifice for mankind tearing down the curtain that separated us from God. So now we enter into God's presence with repentant and humble hearts, but in great earnest and boldness because of the blood of Jesus.

> *Let us then approach God's throne of grace with confidence, so that we may receive mercy and find grace to help us in our time of need.* (Hebrews 4:16)

The summer after I graduated from high school, my oldest brother Eddie and I took a trip to Woodstock for the twenty-fifth anniversary. Mind you, this was a B.C. time in my life (before Christ). The sprawling field where the concerts took place and tents were strewn randomly was blockaded by a large fence keeping unpaid party goers outside the gates. One night during our stay, I was awakened by a roar of people screaming, shouting, and celebrating. The wall was broken down. People were streaming onto the field like ants on peanut butter.

What is my point? Do not leave peanut butter unattended, especially if you have a problem with ants. Okay, that is more of a side point than the main point. The main point is once the fence was broken down, the people were able to charge onto the field with great enthusiasm and boldness. This crowd of unlawful music fans ran with abandoned to indulge themselves in music, mayhem, and Metallica (which is by definition the combination of music and mayhem).

Why is it that sinners can be so bold to sin and righteous people are so shy to approach God with the same unashamed fervor? Jesus has broken down the wall that separated us from God! The veil is torn in two. Our tickets have been paid for by the blood of Jesus Christ. The gates are wide open. The invitation is available to all. "The Spirit and the bride say, 'Come!' And let the one who hears say, 'Come!' Let the one who is thirsty come; and let the one who wishes take the free gift of the water of life" (Revelation 22:17).

God is beckoning us to draw near. Now is the time to approach Him with humility and boldness and Grow Deeper with Him.

Remember my co-worker Rich who I told about Jesus on the first day of work? We became better friends over time, and I continued to share with him the love and truth of Jesus Christ. He even attended Bible studies I held during the lunch hour and often asked me questions about God over the cubical wall. One day at lunch time, I made the invitation for Rich to ask Christ into his life and he accepted the offer. So we went to a local conference room to talk about God and the message of salvation in Jesus Christ. It was in that room that Rich prayed to receive Jesus' love and grace and became "one with the Lord." Praise God!

It's Your Turn

Before time began, God had his eyes on you. He has longed to make you his own and to become one with you in a relationship that is close, intimate, personal and dynamic. Jesus' death on the cross has torn down the barriers of sin that separated you from God. Now you too can "become one with the Lord." So why wait? The invitation is open, the curtains are drawn, the welcome sign is on and God says, "Come to me." It's your turn. Today is the day of salvation, the day you too can become one with God.

Would you pray this prayer with me asking God to make you one with Him?

> *Dear God, I want to be one with you. I want to have an intimate, personal relationship with You. I know my sins have distanced me from you, but I also believe that Jesus' death on the cross paid for my sins to be forgiven. So now God, I ask that you would forgive all my sins, cleanse me and make me one with You. I want to have your life within me and my life found in You. Fill me with Your Holy Spirit and make us one together, inseparable, united, forever and ever, Amen.*

Remember These Truths and Take Action

- It is God's great desire for all of us to Grow Deeper in our relationship with Him to a place of oneness and intimacy.

- God has offered us an opportunity, an open door, for all people to draw near to Him from the heart and to know Him intimately.
- God is beckoning us to draw near. Now is the time to approach Him with humility and boldness and Grow Deeper with Him.
- Jesus has broken down the wall that separated us from God! The veil is torn in two. Our tickets have been paid for by the blood of Jesus Christ. The gates are wide open. The invitation is available to **all**.

Personal Reflection and Group Discussion Questions

- How would you define intimacy with God?
- What would it look like to be one with the Lord?
- What does the prayer life of someone who is close to God look like?
- Think of a time you felt close to God. How would you describe that season of life?

Meditation

God desires me to be close to Him.

Prayer

God, I draw near to You in humility and boldness.

Bible References

- Romans 8:39
- Ephesians 2:8-9
- Titus 3:5
- Genesis 2:24
- Romans 5:10
- Ephesians 1:6
- 1 John 4:9

- 2 Corinthians 13:5
- James 4:8
- Hebrews 9:7
- Exodus 28
- Hebrews 4:14, 16
- Mark 15:28
- 1 Timothy 2:5-6
- Hebrews 7:25
- Psalm 51:17
- Revelation 22:17

Chapter 10

The Friends of Jesus:
How to Be a BFF

I remember the call vividly. It was my nephew Evan.
"Uncle Pierre, I need you to pray."

Anytime a teenager boy gives you a call asking for prayer, you know it must be serious.

"What's up Evan?"

Evan went on to explain how he was out golfing with his father when he, my brother Eddie, fell over on the golf course. Evan was now calling me from the ambulance as they drove my brother to the hospital.

"Yes, let's pray, Evan."

I closed my eyes tightly as I gripped the phone and prayed with all the faith and hope I could muster up.

"Evan, be sure to call me when you know more about his status."

Evan agreed and we both hung up. I immediately sought out my wife who was at home with me and told her what had happened. We again prayed and pleaded with God for my brother's health and life.

Several years earlier, my brother Eddie moved down to Florida for a new job. Well, actually, he thought he was going down for a job, but it was really for something much more important—his sobriety. My brother-in-law Mark had offered him a job at his company just to get him down to Florida and away from the mess he was making of his life in Upstate New York. He was ruining his life and causing great pain to his family by going down the destructive path of drinking and doing drugs. Eddie accepted the offer and not too long after arriving agreed to go into a recovery house.

On only his second visit to my sister Mary and brother-in-law Mark's church, Eddie walked down the aisle to accept Christ into his life.

He described this event saying, "I literally felt the Holy Spirit pick me up out of my seat and carry me down the aisle."

Eddie's conversion was nothing shy of a miracle. Not only did Eddie become sober, he also became a dynamic follower of Jesus Christ. He was constantly glowing with a smile on his face and a positive attitude. "It's all good!" was one of his favorite expressions after coming to Christ.

God had transformed an alcoholic, drug addict, and pusher into a benevolent, kindhearted man who tried to find every opportunity to tell people about Jesus.

My brother's life change had a significant influence on my own spiritual journey. Eddie's amazing testimony and his incredible life transformation was one of the most compelling reasons that brought me to Christ. Something about the dramatic difference in my brother's life, and his testimony of Jesus Christ's love and redemption made me begin to wonder if God was more than a concept or word on a page. Through Eddie, I began to realize that God was alive and able to work and intervene personally in our lives. A few years after Eddie came to Christ, I became a follower of Jesus myself.

After my conversion, my relationship with my brother went to a whole new level. We were already biological blood brothers, but now we were spiritual brothers by the blood of Christ. I could talk to Eddie about any topic in life from heaven to earth and anything in between. We had many passions in common, including sharing Christ with others, especially with our own immediate and extended family.

Receiving Evan's phone call that day was shocking, but I just knew Eddie would be alright. I mean after all, how could his story end now? It was just getting good! Shortly after receiving Evan's call, I received another call from my sister.

She was hysterical, "Eddie is dead. Eddie is dead."

I could not believe my ears. How was this possible? Eddie had fallen over on the golf course that day because of a heart attack and was pronounced dead on arrival at the hospital. He was only forty-two years old.

Only days later, I found myself on an airplane with my wife and our first born son travelling to Florida for his funeral. It was mind boggling how many people we met at the funeral who told about how their lives had been impacted by Eddie's kindness and generosity. Many of these people who I had never met were calling Ed their best friend. Testimony after testimony, story after story told of the good deeds my brother had done, many of them in secret without fanfare. Eddie had made his life count.

One person who had truly been impacted by Eddie was a friend named Dave Hartke. Dave was a friend my brother met who shared the same journey of addiction and recovery. Dave came up to me after the church services and made it clear that he and I were now going to be friends.

"I used to call your brother every day to talk with him. Now that he is gone; I am calling you!"

I did not really know what to make of Dave's proposition, if that is what you would call it. It was more like a declaration or statement of fact. I did not give it much thought after we met not knowing if this guy was serious or just caught up in the moment.

Sure enough, the following week when I was back home in Pennsylvania, I received my first call from Dave. I was glad to connect with him. We both felt the same hole in our hearts as we missed our daily interactions with Eddie. We grieved together and comforted one another. Dave was also a Christian, so he was able to connect with me on a spiritual level just as my brother had been able to previously.

Over the weeks, months and now years, Dave and I have continued to talk each week. He still lives in Florida and I am still in Pennsylvania, but distance does not seem to matter much. In fact, I have not seen Dave more than once or twice since the day of my brother's funeral. Yet I consider him one of my closest and dearest friends. As Dave puts it, "You are my brother from another mother!"

I still miss my brother Eddie to this day. If I could have him back, I would do it in a heartbeat. Although I will not meet Eddie again until heaven, I am so thankful God gave me Dave as a new and close brother. Dave is a confidant; someone I can share my deepest pains and struggles with as well as my ambitions, dreams, and goals in life. He truly is my brother from the same Heavenly Father and a different biological mother. Dave's friendship is one way that I can attest to the fact that God truly does work all things for good, even when we do not have an answer to all the whys of this life.

Something happens when two people share a common spiritual bond with God. Truly we become brothers and sisters through Christ. God has purposed for all those who accept His Son to become a family of believers with God being our Heavenly Father.

> *For whom He foreknew, He also predestined to be conformed to the image of His Son, that He might be the firstborn among many brethren.* (Romans 8:29)

If you have accepted Christ, you are now part of God's worldwide family!

The Brotherhood of Believers

I know that most of the time we refer to Jesus' original followers as disciples and that is what they were. But if you think about it, these guys were more than just students or pupils as the word disciple indicates. They were even more than just friends. They were a brotherhood.

They ate together, travelled together, worked together, and even suffered together. They shared life together.

We all know and have experienced the various levels of relationship. We have friends who are no more than acquaintances, and then we have friends who are more like blood brothers and sisters, sometimes closer than our own blood relatives. We have people who we only talk to about the weather or sports, and then we have people who we can confide in with our deepest fears, concerns, hopes, and dreams. Not everyone can be part of our close knit circle of friends. It does not seem to work that way. At the same time, if we live with only acquaintances and shallow friendships, we will end up feeling lonely and isolated even if we are surrounded by people.

Jesus' Inner Circle

Jesus had twelve disciples, but He had three close friends: Peter, James, and John. These guys were Jesus' three main amigos. As part of Jesus' inner circle of friends, they had special privileges that the others did not. He shared life with these three guys on a deeper level than He did with the other nine. Peter, James, and John were privy to times with Jesus that the other guys were not allowed to experience. They were part of Jesus' inner circle and therefore allowed certain unique rights and privileges.

For instance, Jesus took these three guys up to a high mountain where He was transformed before their very eyes (Matthew 17:1-13). The significance and implication here is profound. For one, Jesus allowed these close friends to know His true identity and self.

Good friends get to know the real you. Good friends are the ones you allow behind the curtain of life to see what is going on backstage.

128

You can tell a good friend who you really are without any masks and without being ashamed. We all need good friends who will love and accept us for who we are when all our guards are down.

Peter, James, and John were with Jesus when He was literally and figuratively on the mountaintop of life. Good friends are never envious of you or jealous of your success. For this reason, you can share your dreams and desires with good friends without reservation because you know they want you to succeed and do well, and will be happy for you when you do. Good friends will support you and cheer you on when you are seeking to be and do your best in life.

My friend Jon Lacrosse is one such friend. Jon and I have met together over the years to talk about life, but also about our specific goals and aspirations. Jon and I keep each other accountable and encourage each other to do our best for the Lord. We pray for each other's success in life. When Jon succeeds I am happy. When I succeed, he is thrilled. We want what's best for one another and aren't out to compete against each other. I thank God for trustworthy, reliable friends like Jon.

Jesus not only invited these three men onto the mountaintop with Him, but also into the valley. It was Peter, James, and John who Jesus escorted with Him to the Garden of Gethsemane before His crucifixion. In this place, they were exposed to Jesus in His weakest and most vulnerable moment. As the scriptures describe it, Jesus was "deeply distressed and troubled" (Mark 14:33). Jesus told these men, "My soul is overwhelmed with sorrow to the point of death" (Mark 14:34).

**Good friends are not just with you on the mountaintop.
Good friends are with you in the valley.**

Good friends can be trusted with your deepest pain, vulnerability, and weakness. Good friends will be at your child's birthday party, but also at your parent's funeral. They are not fair weather friends, they are faithful ones. Jesus trusted Peter, James, and John in the most vulnerable and weakest moment of his life.

All of this may sound good on paper in the same way a romance novel makes love sound effortless and pain free. The reality is that intimate, close friendships require a lot of work and a lot of trust. When all goes well, close friendships pay a huge dividend in this otherwise lonely world. When things go sour, they can cause immeasurable disappointment and pain. Are they worth the risk? Absolutely! Do they come with no strings attached and without any glitches or mishaps? Absolutely not!

As we see from Jesus' story, His closest friends failed Him in His greatest moment of weakness. Instead of staying awake with Him and praying as He asked, these guys fell asleep. In the moment when Jesus needed close friends the most, He found Himself alone. Jesus experienced disappointment in relationships.

"Simon," He said to Peter, "are you asleep? Couldn't you keep watch for one hour?" (Mark 14:37)

Human beings and human friendships will inevitably fail us at some point. When they do, we have a choice to make. Do we give up on those friends and find new ones? Do we give up on close friendships all together and trust no one? Or, do we do like Jesus did and choose to be the best friend we can be to others and encourage them on their journey of faith?

To truly Grow Together with others means we learn how to love other people in spite of their obvious weaknesses, frailties, and failures.

If anyone had the right to condemn people and walk away disappointed and even angry, it was Jesus. Yet, that is not what He did.

He stuck it out and He kept being the faithful friend even unto death. "Greater love has no one than this: to lay down one's life for one's friends" (John 15:13). When it comes to Growing Together with others, the ultimate question is not how many good and close friends you can accumulate, but rather how you can become a good and faithful friend to others. Even Jesus' closest friends were not able to remain faithful in His greatest moment of need. Do not be surprised or enraged if your own friends disappoint you.

Instead, look inside your own heart and ask yourself these questions:

Am I a faithful friend?

Can I be a trustworthy confidant to others in need?

Am I happy when my friends succeed without feeling covetous, envious or jealous?

Will I make myself vulnerable to others and risk my heart even when I have no guarantee of their loyalty or trust?

BFF – Best Friends Forever

Growing Together requires us to open our hearts at the risk of being hurt. Jesus had many people who knew Him and were acquaintances. He had twelve friends who followed Him around for three years. He had three close friends in Peter, James, and John. Then, among the three close disciples, Jesus had one who was His closest friend. He is referred to as "the disciple whom Jesus loved" (John 13:23). Bible scholars as well as church historians agree this refers to the Apostle John, the son of Zebedee and brother of James. John had the privilege of being Jesus' best friend in His time on earth. In the world of text messaging, John was Jesus' "BFF"—Best Friend Forever.

As Jesus' best friend, John was entrusted with a greater level of intimacy and openness from Jesus' heart than the other disciples. He was allowed the honor of knowing Christ in anonymity and privacy. He was close to Jesus' heart. John and Jesus had a level of intimacy in their friendship that the other disciples never knew. It was John who was leaning next to Jesus during the last meal Jesus ate before His death. It was John who stood by Jesus' side even unto death when the other disciples had run away scared. It was John who Jesus entrusted with the care of His own mother (John 19:26).

How was John privileged with the great honor of being Jesus' best friend? Did all the guys draw straws and John pulled the longest one out? Just my opinion, but I do not think it went down that way. I believe that Jesus *chose* John to be His best friend because of something He saw in him. "The righteous should choose his friends carefully" (Proverbs 12:26a NKJV).

The fact that Jesus asked John to take care of His mother Mary after His death tells us a lot about John, also known as the "Apostle of Love." For one thing, John was reliable. You just do not give the care of someone you love, especially your own mother, to someone who is not faithful to their commitments. John had obviously proven to Jesus that he was a dependable, trustworthy, and reliable man.

In fact, John's presence at the cross was an indicator of his faithful commitment to Jesus. Peter was off singing with the roosters. You could hear Judas walking away with thirty pieces of silver jingling in his pocket. John, on the other hand, was a faithful friend, sticking with Jesus to the bitter end of His life.

John was not only trustworthy; he also had an amazingly tender heart. I do not know about you, but when I think of someone who I want to share with on a deep level, I am looking to avoid those who are sarcastic, cynical, critical, and harsh. I want someone who has a soft heart, a humble spirit, and a kindness about them that makes me feel safe. John was cuddled up next to Jesus' side at the last supper. He had a heart that was soft and moldable.

**Best friends are like good mattresses. They need to be soft
enough to provide comfort, but firm enough to provide support.**

John was both. If you examine John's writings, you see that John
was not afraid to tell the truth. "If we say that we have no sin, we
deceive ourselves, and the truth is not in us" (1 John 1:8). You can sense
a stark contrast in John's ability to speak truthfully, but also be loving
and tender.

Close friends are not afraid to tell you the truth even when it
hurts. "Faithful are the wounds of a friend" (Proverbs 27:6a KJV). A
good friend will warn you when you are crossing a street of life without
looking for oncoming traffic. A good friend will pop your bubble of
pride, not to see you fall, but to make sure you do not get too high
before the inevitable fall comes. On a lighter note, as my sister Mary
has said, "A good friend will tell you if you have food stuck in your
teeth." My sister Michele adds, "or goop on your nose." The bottom
line is that good friends are honest even when the truth is painful
because they know that truth is our ultimate friend.

If you truly desire to live a life that emulates Christ, you must seek
to develop close and intimate friendships just as Jesus did with His disciples, the inner circle three, and with John, his BFF. Similar to Jesus,
let us seek to have a group of friends we spend time with, a group of
people we feel closer to, and a select person or maybe two we share with
at a deep and intimate level about every aspect of life.

As I close this chapter, our little puppy Angel came into my room
and sat by my chair. She wanted to be next to me and probably was
looking for a little scratch on the belly. The camaraderie of dogs has
won them the title of "man's best friend." It is companionship and
what the Bible calls "fellowship" that our hearts truly long for in this
life. We all want someone who will come by our side to be *with* us on

the journey. It is not always a physical presence, like my good friend Dave in Florida who is miles away every time we speak. Instead, it is a heart to heart connection that transcends time and space between two people who love one another from the depths of their soul, and are committed to each other to the end of life.

Remember These Truths and Take Action

- God has purposed for all those who accept His Son to become a family of believers with God being our Heavenly Father.
- You can tell a good friend who you really are without any masks and without being ashamed. We all need good friends who will love and accept us for who we are when all our guards are down.
- To truly "Growing Together" with others means we learn how to love other people in spite of their obvious weaknesses, frailties, and failures.
- When it comes to Growing Together with others, the ultimate question is not how many good and close friends you can accumulate, but rather how you can become a good and faithful friend to others.

Personal Reflection and Group Discussion Questions

- What characteristics are most important to you in a best friend?
- What challenges do you face in letting others see the real you?
- How would you define trust? What makes trust vital to close relationships?
- How can you work on becoming a better friend to others?

Meditation

God desires for me to have close friends.

Prayer

God, give me good friends and help me to be one.

Bible References

- Matthew 17:1-13
- Mark 14:33-14
- Mark 14:37
- John 15:13
- John 13:23
- John 19:26
- Proverbs 12:26a
- 1 John 1:8
- Proverbs 27:6a

Chapter 11

Here's the Church.
Here's the Steeple.

Have you ever played the game of word association? Here is how it works. I will write a word. After you read the word, you need to respond with the very first word that comes to your mind. Are you ready? You can say the word aloud or write it on the blank line next to the word. Here we go.

Black. _____

Ebony. _____

Big. _____

Car._____

Church._____

Now, let me take my best guess at your responses. You said, "White, Ivory, Little, Truck, and ...." I am curious, what did you say after you read "Church"? Since I cannot be transported through these pages to sit next to you and have a conversation, I am going to have to take a guess at what you might have said. Boy, you are really going to make me work hard for this, aren't you?

Okay, here goes nothing. I will give myself three guesses. I am guessing you either said, Steeple, Building, or....hold on one second. My Mom is calling me. I will give her this same set of words...

My Mom said, "White, Ivory, Small, What type of car are you talking about? Then she said, "Oh, God."

At first I was not sure if she was upset with me when she said, "Oh, God" or if God was her answer and the "Oh" was just a pause before the answer.

"Is that your final answer, Mom?" I asked her.

"Yes," she said, "It is God."

Okay, so now based on my empirical data, my guess is that you said Steeple, Building or God. Okay, did I guess right? I guess I will never know. I will try not to let the suspense get the best of me.

Do you remember this old nursery rhyme? Here's the church, here's the steeple, open it up, and see all the people. It came with accompanying hand motions—interlocked fingers, then two fingers pointing up for steeples, then inversed, and wiggly fingers for all the people. Man, that church was packed out! They should really consider starting a second service!

If I could change the world, peanut butter and milk chocolate would become a basic food group, and the words of that rhyme would go something like this, "Here is a building and here is a steeple, if you open it up you see the church—God's people!

The word translated as "church" in our Bible comes from a Greek word *ekklesia* that means "called out." To add some more sustenance, called out really refers to *people* who are called out. To go a step further, these are people called out *by God*. To dive even deeper, we understand this group of people to be those who have been called out by God *from darkness into light*. The people who are called out by God from darkness into light have *an ordained purpose for their existence* here on earth. To take it one final step further, this group of people is meant to be a *supportive community* that Grows Together, and becomes stronger as a whole being fortified against all opposition as they work to achieve God's greater purposes in the world.

Jesus said, "I will build my church (*ekklesia*), and the gates of Hades will not overcome it" (Matthew 16:18). When Jesus said He was going to build His church, He was not talking about a building project. He was not looking to run a capital funds financial campaign. He did not mean building a program, a once a week dynamic church service or a weekly Bible study. He was not talking about building a worldwide religion either. He did not have church hierarchy in mind with various levels of governing authority.

Jesus was talking about building and developing a group of people, God's people.

But you are a chosen people, a royal priesthood, a holy nation, God's special possession, that you may declare the praises of him who called you out of darkness into his wonderful light. (1 Peter 2:9)

Going back to the word association game, I think the word most closely associated with the true meaning of church according to God's Word is "community." God's church is truly meant to be a community of people who all have one main thing and many other smaller related things in common.

The one main thing we share together is the fact that God, through Christ, has called us out of darkness to Himself and we are now His people, His possession, and His reward.

We are God's chosen ones! Along with the one main thing in common come many other important commonalities like our identity, our purpose, our future, our hope, our calling, and our eternal destiny. We have more in common than we would often like to admit! The early church did the community thing really well. Listen to the way church sounded in those days.

They devoted themselves to the apostles' teaching and to fellowship, to the breaking of bread and to prayer. Everyone was filled with awe at the many wonders and signs performed by the apostles. All the believers were together and had everything in common. They sold property and possessions to give to anyone who had need. Every day they continued to meet together in the temple courts. They broke bread in their homes and ate together with glad and sincere hearts, praising God and enjoying the favor of all the people. And the Lord added to their number daily those who were being saved. (Acts 2:42-47)

I have heard people occasionally say things like, "I just want to be part of a New Testament church." While I understand and appreciate this desire, I am not sure if people really understand what they are asking for, and if they would be willing to sacrifice to get it. In fact, I think what we really want are the *results* of the New Testament church more than living the way the New Testament church lived. Wonders, signs, God's favor, and numerous salvations sound awesome to me, too! Sign me up!

But wait a minute; did you notice what it took to get to that place? First of all, it took the undisputable power of the Holy Spirit. Let's just get that straight right from the start. Nothing good was happening without God's empowering presence. Beyond stating the obvious need for God's intervention and empowerment, we need to look at what the people themselves contributed to this heavenly equation.

The first observation is that these people were devoted. "*They devoted themselves...*" The word devoted comes from a Greek word *proskartereo* that means to persevere and continue on. The people of God were persistent and regular in their study of the Apostles' teaching (today's Bible study), in fellowship (interacting with each other), breaking of bread (eating and taking communion), and prayer.

I am no handy man. In fact, anytime something in my house breaks it becomes a new opportunity for a miracle from God. "Please God, help me to get this fixed!" My good friend, neighbor, brother-in-Christ, and handyman Mark Marshall is coming to my house today to help fix a few things for me. Thank God for Christian community! (Mark, you are a good man!)

One of the most annoying and fairly common house issues I have faced in times past is a leaky faucet. I have had several in my days as a homeowner and currently, knock on granite counter tops, I have none. Halleluiah, Jesus is alive! What annoys me more than not knowing how to fix a leaky faucet is the sound of continually dripping—Drip. Drop. Drip. Drop. Somebody stop the madness!

When the early church met together, they did so with drip drop consistency. On paper, it does not sound too challenging any more than a leaky faucet does to my friend Mark Marshall. In reality, however, the meeting together with other believers in Jesus on a consistent and even daily basis would be enough to make many of us wish we had a leaky faucet to go fix. "Sorry guys, got to run! I think I hear my faucet leaking!"

Fellowship and community to the early church was more than a cup of coffee and some donuts after a weekend church service.

"How's your coffee?"
"Great."
"Enjoy your donut."
"See you next week."

Instead, it was a consistent and continual living together with one another in a drip, drop, every day kind of way. The early church was devoted to meeting with one another as if their spiritual lives depended on it.

My second stark observation is how these people shared with one another. *"All the believers were together and had everything in common."* As author and Pastor Craig Groeschel coined it in his book, "It," these people had "refrigerator rights" in each other's homes. Refrigerator rights are what family members and close friends have together. You can walk into the house, open the refrigerator without asking, and take what you want. You have got the rights! In the early church, it seemed to work that way. People were opening one another's refrigerators and sharing what was inside. "Look, it's meatloaf!"

Now is when it gets a bit too uncomfortable for our Western appetite. Here is my fair warning to you. This next portion of scripture will challenge you down to your independent, retirement building core. If there was any time to find a leaky faucet in your house, now is it! Bail now before the conviction rolls in.

"They sold property and possessions to give to anyone who had need" (v.45).

Are you still there?

Hello. Is anybody home?

Mom, it looks like it is just you and me at this point; everyone else has sprung a leak!

When I mentioned community earlier in this chapter, I know what some of you were thinking—pot luck dinners, picnics after church, cole slaw, corn on the cob, and watermelon. Oh the joy of community! Yes, food is an essential aspect of community for sure. The early church definitely had food as part of their gatherings. I am sure it added an important ingredient to their community gatherings. Before we get distracted by the smell of fresh baked bread, let's realize that real community goes a lot deeper than our digestive tract. It can actually go as deep as our pocketbooks, bank accounts, and 401k plans.

Hello? Is anybody still there?

Let me put this another way that may help you digest this hard truth. Let's use baseball as an example. It is the bottom of the ninth with one out. The game is tied, you are up to bat and you have one runner on third base. All you need to do is get that runner home and you win the game. What do you need to do in order to score the winning run? That's right – hit a "Sacrifice Fly."

Now if you are not familiar with baseball, let me clarify that a Sacrifice Fly is not the offering you give if you cannot afford a pure, spotless lamb. A Sacrifice Fly is when you hit the ball up in the air to the outfield knowing that you yourself will get out, but your teammate who is on base will be able to advance to the next base or even come home and score.

In true Christian community, what the Bible refers to as church, sacrificial flies are a regular part of the game. In other words, people do things for one another and give things to one another in a way that exhausts their own resources of time, talent, energy, and even money. There is a good reason for this sharing of life and resources. It is not just to take one for the team or to make others feel good. It is not even to make yourself feel good about what you have done to help another person out and build your self-esteem.

True community takes place because the people do not see themselves as individual units who happen to be in the same room together. Instead they see themselves as being one unit, one organism, one body united together.

The Apostle Paul, in relaying the importance of unity in God's church to the believers in Corinth, said it this way, "If one part suffers, every part suffers with it; if one part is honored, every part rejoices with it. Now you are the body of Christ, and each one of you is a part of it" (1 Corinthians 12:26-27). We are one body with many parts. Each part plays a role in the body and no part is independent of the whole.

The Pointer Finger Crisis

Two weeks ago I was doing some hedge trimming in my back yard again. Do not worry; I did not take down any bird's nests this time! Instead, I mistook my pointer finger for a tree branch and had a pretty severe gash on the tip of my finger. When it happened, my whole body responded in unison to help salvage my finger tip. My brain shot out signals to my entire body to respond to this emergency.

Instantly, my body began to respond to my brain's signals. My right hand grabbed my finger to minimize the blood loss and keep my finger in place. My feet went on high speed and ran me back into my house. My mouth started ushering out commands to my kids. "Quick find Mommy!" My face showed signs of panic that worried my little daughter Olivia (sorry, sweetheart!). My shoulder held the phone in place as I dialed 911. The whole body was working together just to help my little bitty fingertip stay intact. By God's grace, my wife drove me to the hospital in time to salvage my finger. Now two weeks later, the nine stitches have been removed and my finger is back into action working fine.

T.G.F.F.F. – Thank God for Five Fingers!

So what is my point? My point is that my entire body came into play in order to rescue my itsy, bitsy finger tip. It was a team effort! My brain, feet, eyes, right hand, and even my heart and lungs were all working together to help save and rescue my finger. It was a microcosm of community at its finest.

As God calls us to Grow Together, He has in mind a functioning body, similar to your physical body. In this body, every person has a function and purpose and no part of the body is more important than the rest with only one exception – the head.

Going back to my story of the almost lost finger, remember that it was my brain or head that initiated the save and rescue mission of Mr. Pointer Finger. The head shot off the commands, "You feet, get moving. Mouth start communicating. Eyes, keep yourself focused and headed in the right direction." The brain was unquestionably the most valuable member of the entire team.

So who is this all important head of the church body? Is it the pastor? The priest? The Bishops? The Pope? No, No, No, and No. The head of the body is Christ.

And he (Jesus) is the head of the body, the church; he is the beginning and the firstborn from among the dead, so that in everything he might have the supremacy. (Colossians 1:18)

Jesus is not only the master builder of this thing we call church, He is the head of the community as well. Jesus is the one who is ultimately calling the shots for the body of Christ to follow. Each one of us is considered members of His beautiful body. I am not talking about church membership here. I am talking about being joined together with a worldwide community of Christ followers where He plays the role of the head, the brain, and the leader. We are His hands, feet, arms, neck, and even left hand pointer fingers.

Now getting back to the early church and the community they developed together, we see that these people did not just call one another by familial names. "Good morning, Brother Jim." "God bless you, Sister Samantha." The people in the New Testament actually lived together as if they were family. They shared rights, privileges, finances, houses, cars...well they did not really have cars back then, but you get the point. They shared their entire lives with one another!

As a result, God showed this group of Jesus loving people great favor, power, and grace. Miracles took place. People were healed. Others were delivered. Many were saved and the church (community of people) grew together rapidly, yes even daily! Now, that is good stuff! It is what every sincere believer in Christ longs to see—a church that is alive, well, and growing to the glory of God!

The early church enjoyed this God given success and favor. They ate together. They were happy. They were thankful. They were praising God and enjoying His goodness. It sounds a lot like Thanksgiving! People gathering together and celebrating all God was doing in their lives and giving thanks for it. I think I would really enjoy some church like that, how about you?

Church is meant to be so much more than a building and a steeple. The church is intended to be a community of God's people gathering together to celebrate all the Lord has done. It is to regularly, yes even daily, come together to Grow Deeper in the knowledge of God and

His will for their lives. This family of believers is not just focused on their own needs, but on meeting the needs of one another and on reaching the world around them with the love, truth, and grace of God the Father found in Jesus Christ.

Now that is church! So, my friend, let me ask you a question, "When was the last time you experienced true church?" I am not talking about the last time you went into a building we call church. That is important, too, but it is by no means the sum of what God intended for His people, His family. My question has to do more with whether or not you are actually Growing Together with a group of people who love God, and love one another in a way that is more akin to a family reunion than just a rock concert or funeral or any other style of worship that may fit somewhere in between.

Hard Work and Sacrifice

Now before we run off with the notion that the church is just one big happy family, we must come to grips with the reality that family, community, and church as God meant it to be requires a lot of hard work. It takes work and sacrifice, especially considering the busy nature of our lives these days, to make time for and to live out healthy Christian community. Is it even worth all the hassle? I mean, can we just stick to going to "church" on Sunday morning and then live a normal unbothered life Monday through Saturday? Do we really need this whole community thing? Can we just keep church more placid and safe? Do we really have to get involved in one another's lives to the degree described in the Bible?

The honest truth is that you do not really have to do community like God describes or prescribes. You have the God given right to choose the safe path, the non-communal, non-committal, and non-invasive form of "church."

That is your choice. God will not take it away from you. It is just not the best option. Living a life that is independent and free of all the messiness of community, people, conflict, issues, and sacrifice is certainly an option that you can take. Many people willingly or in ignorance choose this path. Sometimes the hurt of past "church" issues keep people at arm's length from living in real community.

A guy once said to me, "Forget church. It is all about a personal relationship with Jesus."

Sorry, wrong answer. Try and find that in the New Testament. (Hint: it's not there!) Other times, people never have the concept of community in mind when they hear the word church. They simple associate the word church with a building you go once a week, a place you go when someone dies, gets married or on Christmas and Easter. They hear "church" and think of a white building with a steeple on top.

Now you can no longer say you have not heard of church as a community of believers. Sorry, I ruined that for you. The good news is you still have a choice. You have the choice to keep it simple and keep it clean. You can do "church" once a week or month or whatever frequency you can find time to make it to the building on Sunday without having community and sharing life with others. If that is your choice, it is your prerogative. Just do yourself and God a favor. **Do not call it church.** If church is reduced down to a weekly ritual, like doing laundry on Saturday morning, it no longer earns the right to be called church. Give it another title. Call it Drive-Thru Spirituality or One and Done Christianity or maybe See-You-in-a-week-until-then-we-won't-speak or maybe we could cut that short to See-You-Next-Someday. Whatever you do, just do not call it church. It would be a misnomer. It would be like playing the word association game and saying "Ivory" after you hear "Car." It just does not fit.

Jesus is working to build His church, His community, His people into a strong, growing, vibrant, and healthy family that Grows Up, Grows Out, and Grows Deeper all Together as one unit.

He is calling you and me to join together in partnership with a local group of other Christ followers to be the church, His representation here on earth for others to witness and experience God's goodness through us. The challenge for each of us is being willing to commit to other people, live sacrificially, and love one another affectionately in a way that models to the watching world what it means to be one of God's own children.

- *Will you accept the challenge to Grow Together with other believers in a community of faith?*
- *Will you dive into the work of God with those around you?*
- *Will you be content with whatever part of the body you get to play, even if it is not the role everyone admires?*
- *Will you commit to Growing Together with other believers to make God's church grow stronger?*

I know at this point it sounds more like a wedding ceremony than anything else. "Will you Jack take Jill to be your lawfully wedded wife? Will you honor her, cherish her....?" You are right! Church is much more like a marriage covenant between a man and a woman. It takes commitment and sacrifice. That is why it is so hard to find, but why it is also so worth going after and worth treasuring once you have it.

The next time you hear or say the word "church", remember it is not about buildings, choirs, robes, crosses, steeples, fish bumper stickers or any other Christian paraphernalia.

**Church is about people, God's people, living together
in a way that builds one another up, and works together
to see a lost world find Jesus.**

God is calling each of us to Grow Together by finding a group of believers we treat as family and committing to serve one another, love one another, encourage one another, and every other "one another" found in scripture. You just cannot do that sitting next to people you do not know in a building you call "church". This type of church takes hard work, sacrifice, love, and intentionality. Church like this is so important to God, He was willing to allow Jesus to die for it. Do not miss out on being an active part of God's body, the church!

Remember These Truths and Take Action

- When Jesus said He was going to build His church, He was talking about developing a group of people, God's people.
- God's church is truly meant to be a community of people who share life together.
- In true Christian community, what the Bible refers to as church, sacrifice is the norm.
- As God calls us to Grow Together, He has in mind a functioning body, similar to your physical body. In this body, every person has a function and purpose, and no part of the body is more important than the rest with only one exception—the head, Jesus.
- The church is intended to be a community of God's people gathering together regularly to celebrate all that the Lord has done, and to Grow Deeper in the knowledge of God and His will for their lives.

- Church is about people, God's people, living together in a way that builds one another up and works together to see a lost world find Jesus.

Personal Reflection and Group Discussion Questions

- When you think of "church" what is the first word that comes to your mind?
- What are the implications of viewing church more as a community than a place you go each week?
- What groups of people can you think of that demonstrate sacrificial, communal living?
- What are the advantages and disadvantages of "doing church" without developing true community?

Meditation

Church is a community of people, not a physical building.

Prayer

God, help me to develop true community with other believers.

Bible References

- 1 Peter 2:9
- Acts 2:42-47
- 1 Corinthians 12:26-27
- Colossians 1:18

Chapter 12

There Is Room for Growth!

I used to love school shopping as a kid. The school supplies were not the thrill; I enjoyed getting new clothes. As a young sprouting boy, my Mom knew that by the end of the school year I would have outgrown most of my clothing. So in motherly wisdom she would make me buy clothes that were a little bigger so I would have some "room to grow." That way I would not be wearing high waters by the time the school year ended—ingenious!

I had some of my greatest growth spurts as a teenager. Along with a growing body, I had an equally healthy appetite. I could eat a full dinner and then half an hour later feel hungry and woof down a couple bowls of cereal. It is a wonder my parents never had to take out loans just to feed us six kids!

Like any good parents, my Mom and Dad were happy when I grew, not just physically of course, but also in maturity, responsibility, and character. All good parents want their kids to grow up and mature, and love to tell others about the progress their kids are making.

God the Father is no different. He has bought you some really big shoes to fit into; they are size "Jesus." He knows you have room to grow and wants to see you fit into the same size shoes as your older brother Jesus. His food budget has no limit. He has enough provision to get you to the place He longs for you to be in Christ. You are the topic of conversation in heaven. He boasts to the angels about you. "Look at my kids! Watch them grow!"

As we bring our time together to a close, I want you to again consider the four directions in life that God is calling you to grow, and how the Father eagerly desires for you to reach your fullest potential in Christ. For truly, there is still room for you to grow in Christ!

Growing Up

I did not have affection towards babies until I had my own children. That is when I became a big time baby fan. I love babies. I love their vulnerability and innocence. I love their smell after a good baby bath. I love their soft and squishy skin.

As cute, wonderful, and precious as my own three children Elijah, Jordan, and Olivia were as babies, I knew that they all needed to grow up. Waking up in the middle of the night, changing messy diapers, and inconsolable cries during sickness are not things my wife or I miss about that phase of life.

One thing I do miss, however, is feeding my kids from a bottle. There was something special for me as a Dad to hold that bottle to their mouth and see them suck down the milk with intensity and fervor. You could just sense how hungry and how appreciative they were of that milk. They were even defensive over those bottles of liquid lactose. Take it away and you would think someone sounded a fire alarm!

I also enjoyed feeding them baby food. Something in my conservative, frugal nature loved to scoop up the peas and carrot puree as it dribbled down their chin and shove it right back into their mouths—not a teaspoon wasted! It did not take long to see the cause and effect of all their bottle drinking and baby food eating. Babies not only know how to drink and eat; babies know how to grow! If you want to see a baby grow all you need to do is nourish her with the right food and drink, give her the appropriate amount of rest and *"Ba-da-boom"*–your baby grows faster than a Ch-Ch-Ch-Chia Pet*!

God the Father loves to feed us and He also loves to see us grow. God loves it when we hunger after His Spirit and drink the milk of His Word.

Like newborn babies, crave pure spiritual milk, so that by it you may grow up in your salvation. (1 Peter 2:2)

God wants us to grow up strong and healthy and so He tells us plainly, "Keep hungering after My Word." If we do, the promise is clear, we will grow up in our salvation, meaning we will start to look like the one who saved us, Jesus. Do not ever stop hungering after the Word of God.

Do not just eat up God's Word without also drinking in His Spirit. Eating only the Word without also filling up with the Spirit is like trying to eat Saltine crackers without having any water. You will get dry and pasty real quick. Do not become spiritually dehydrated. Take a deep drink of the Holy Spirit. Just say to God, "Fill me afresh with Your Holy Spirit!" and He will.

Eating God's Word and drinking deeply of the Holy Spirit in prayer and praise will inevitably result in spiritual growth. God's Word never returns back void and His Spirit always cultivates life and godliness within us.

You cannot help but grow up if you persistently and consistently read the Bible, pray, and invite the Holy Spirit to take control of your life. You are bound to grow, grow, grow up, and away!

Growing Out

I was driving my boys to our church early one Sunday morning a few weeks ago. It was my weekend to preach and we were running late. Running late to church is always a fun test of your Christian faith, especially when you are the preacher!

My children have been anointed by the Holy Spirit to convict me of fast driving.

"Dad, what's the speed limit and how fast are you going?"

I try to ignore them, but they are persistent.

"Dad, what's the speed limit and how fast are you going?"

After their constant badgering I decided I would slow down, go the speed limit and trust God with my arrival time. I figured that lying to my kids before I preached was probably worse than arriving a few minutes late to church.

As God's grace would have it, that day I hit all green lights! My boys were astonished.

"Dad, every light we come to is turning green, even as we are approaching them!"

I do not know about you, but I sure do appreciate getting green lights and going forward so much more than stopping at red lights—especially when I am running late! This particular morning God was working things for my good in a very practical, green kind of way. Thank you, Jesus! (Mark 16:15).

When it comes to sharing our faith with the world around us, Jesus has given us one big, fat green light. He said to His disciples, "Go into all the world and preach the gospel to all creation."

Jesus has given us a green light to be a light unto the world. Do not slow down now, go, go, go into all the world and tell people about Jesus!

In the kingdom of God so many truths work in paradox to our natural world and senses. For example, God's green light was preceded by a yellow light and before that a red light. Jesus told His disciples, "And now I will send the Holy Spirit, just as my Father promised. But **stay here in the city** until the Holy Spirit comes and fills you with power from heaven" (Luke 24:49, NLT). Jesus was giving His followers a red light. Do not go anywhere yet, boys, just "stay here in the city."

I am writing this final chapter from a beach house in Ocean City, New Jersey. My friend Mike Hutchinson Sr. and his wife Sue were kind enough to loan my family their beach home for a few days of R & R. (Thank you, Mike and Sue!)

I have a two point checklist before any long car ride. First is to make sure my kids empty their bladder and second is to make sure my gas tank gets filled. Now that is fatherly wisdom at its finest! Before we packed the van and headed to the shore, I made a pit stop at the local gas station to fill up my tank. I always prefer to start the trip with a full tank of gas so I do not need to make any unnecessary stops along the way. I am no mechanic, but one thing I have learned from my own experience is that when your vehicle runs out of gas, you are not going anywhere. Every vehicle needs fuel in order to move forward.

Jesus told His disciples to stop before they went on their journey into the world and to wait "until the Holy Spirit comes and fills you with power from heaven." Jesus was telling us to make sure we keep our tank full before we head out the door and into the world. Waiting for the Holy Spirit to come and fill you with power from heaven is God's yellow light so to speak.

I can be a pretty impatient person, but when I am at the gas station, I know enough not to pull away before I hear the "click" sound of the trigger indicating that my tank is filled. In the same vein, when we allow ourselves to wait in God's presence daily and also patiently listen to the Spirit's promptings as we dialogue with people who are not yet followers of Christ, God fills us with power and strength to share Jesus in a way that is energized and dynamic.

Stop; wait on the Holy Spirit, then go!

Growing Deeper

I am about to take a break from my writing for a moment to walk my kids down to the shore. Fortunately, my kids are all good swimmers and enjoy the water. My oldest son, Elijah has the most swimming experience and is the best swimmer followed by his younger brother, Jordan, and then my daughter, Olivia.

The depth I allow each of my kids to go into the ocean is based on their individual maturity level and swimming ability. The more mature they are, the farther they are allowed to go because with maturity comes corresponding permission and opportunity, not to mention responsibility. As their father, I am always trying to coach each one to go a little bit deeper and grow in their swimming skills.

God the Father is a good parent. He does not want us to sink, drown, and lose our faith. God is always looking for us to go deeper into the sea of His loving grace. He wants us to have a deep, abiding relationship with Him that empowers us not only to swim in the deep end of the pool, but to walk on water out in the open sea.

When my wife and I were dating, we took a trip to Florida to see both sides of our family. We started in Boca Raton visiting my sister and brother. My brother-in-law Mark loaned us his brand spanking new BMW to take a trip from Boca to visit Amanda's grandmother who lived in Orlando.

This car was completely loaded with everything imaginable—a built-in phone system, individualized air conditioning, leather seats—you name it, it had it. The coolest feature about this car was that it had a built in GPS system. Nowadays this is common place, but at that time it was a novelty.

My brother-in-law punched in the address of our destination to the car's GPS and we took off over the river and through the woods to Grandma Augusta's house in Or-lan-do. Driving under the direction of an automated voice was a step of faith for a guy like me who was used to following maps and hand written directions. I willingly set aside my Ponce de León instincts and listened to the melodic sounds of the woman inside the dashboard. "In 200 feet, turn left." "Okay, ma'am, whatever you say."

Now if you are at all familiar with Florida, you know that a trip from Boca to Orlando is pretty much a straight shot North. Over

140 miles of the slightly more than 200 mile trip is spent driving straight up the Florida Turnpike.

As we started off on the journey, Ms. GPS gave me the instructions to get on the Turnpike. Then not long after, she told me to take an exit. So being a good student and listener, I followed her instructions. She led us to I-95 North. We got on I-95 and after going a few miles north were again directed back to the Florida Turnpike. Moments later, she changed her mind and told us to exit off the Turnpike. Guess where she told us to go? You guessed it, back to I-95.

Now I have never claimed to be the smartest guy in the world, but on this particular day my stupidity capacity was running on a full tank. This mysterious woman who I had just met had me zigzagging my way up the peninsula of Florida. I now realize what GPS *really* stands for—Gauging Pierre's Stupidity!

After about the fourth trip back and forth between the Florida Turnpike and I-95, I scratched my head and realized these roads were parallel to one another and there was no good reason to split my time between them. I fired Ms. GPS and put Mr. Cerebral back in charge. I was not going to waste any more time; I was going to take the straight route to Orlando!

On this journey of faith we have one common destination. His name is Jesus. Jesus is our end goal. Jesus is not only the final stop on the journey; He is also the path along the journey as well. He told Thomas, "I am the way" (John 14:6a).

Too often, we get distracted and end up zigzagging in life to the left and the right instead of seeking God's final answer, path and destination—Jesus the Christ.

The writer of the book of Hebrews put it this way,

Therefore, since we are surrounded by such a great cloud of witnesses, let us throw off everything that hinders and the sin that so easily entangles. And let us run with perseverance the race marked out for us, fixing our eyes on Jesus, the pioneer and perfecter of faith. For the joy set before him he endured the cross, scorning its shame, and sat down at the right hand of the throne of God. Consider him who endured such opposition from sinners, so that you will not grow weary and lose heart. (Hebrews 12:1-3)

Friend, if you want the quickest way to grow closer to God, you need to fix your eyes on the person of Jesus, and run your hardest to Him forsaking all other distractions no matter how good they may look, feel or sound. Sin, Satan, and sensual desires can lead us astray from the finish line of our faith, the person of Jesus Christ.

Sometimes even "Christian" things have a way of leading us to every place other than Jesus Himself. Program "Jesus" into your spiritual guidance system, and do not waste your time looking to the left or right!

If the counsel you receive, the books you read, the sermons you hear or the revelations you experience do not lead you back to the person of Jesus, they will only zig-zag you along in life until you are all out of spiritual gas.

Growing Together

On another car ride in Florida my college friends and I were packed together into a little Mitsubishi Spyder convertible that we rented for the week of our Spring Break. Somewhere along the ride one of us had the brilliant idea of playing "The Heat Game" in the car.

Now if you have never heard of The Heat Game let me briefly explain how this idiotic game works. You roll up all the windows of your vehicle (and in our case also close the convertible top) and you then turn on the car's heat full blast. As you can imagine, the heat index in the car intensifies until the point where you feel like you are in a mobile sauna. The game ends when the first person in the vehicle calls out for mercy and says, "Turn off the heat!"

We drove in the car that Floridian hot sunny day feeling absolutely miserable with beads of sweet pouring down our heads. We were laughing and joking along the way as we suffered together. Misery truly does love company. Finally my roommate and friend Zack Grice shouted out, "I give up! Turn off the heat!" Immediately the heat was shut off, the windows were rolled down, and the roof was opened wide. We were saved from the heat! Talk about the joy of salvation!

We then all took turns poking fun at Zack for being the quitter and giver-upper. Truthfully, Zack may have been the first to quit, but that is only because he was the smartest guy inside our four wheel Spyder. (Zack proved his intellectual brilliance by being named valedictorian at our graduation ceremony the following May. You, go Zack! We knew you had it all along.)

What is the moral of the story? College kids do stupid things! No, there is another more important moral to this story as well. If you ever make the foolish choice to play The Heat Game[8] make sure you have someone in the car who is smart enough to say, "Turn off the heat!"

No honestly, here is the true moral of the story—life is done better together. As painful and miserable as the heat ride from hell was, it did something to draw us closer together and bond us as friends. The refreshing breeze of air flowing through the sports car that day brought each of us refreshment individually. Experiencing this refreshment together brought even greater delight and joy.

The Christ following life is filled with many joys and many pains. It is filled with times of laughter, times of sorrow, times of pain and loss, and times of incredible blessings and joys. At times you will feel like

---

[8] Please note that I do not under any circumstances advice or endorse playing "The Heat Game." Just learn from our example that this game is dumb and foolish. It will save you a lot of blood, sweat, and tears.

God is playing The Heat Game in your life, and you are not sure why everything seems to be so uncomfortable and pain-filled. Other times, you will feel like you are driving a ten-speed bike downhill with the refreshing air blowing on your face. Life will be a breeze and you will be getting along with ease.

In any and every season of life, the journey is always sweeter when the road you travel is not traversed alone because God has called us to Grow Together.

We are to grow together in pain. We are to grow together in joy. We are to grow together in laughter. We are to grow together in sorrow. Solomon said, "Two are better than one, because they have a good return for their labor: If either of them falls down, one can help the other up. *But pity anyone who falls and has no one to help them up.*" (Ecclesiastes 4:9-10)

Before Jesus ended His journey on earth, He spoke to His Father on behalf of His friends and followers. "I will remain in the world no longer, but they are still in the world, and I am coming to you. Holy Father, protect them by the power of your name, the name you gave me, so that they may be one as we are one" (John 17:11).

Jesus' final prayer was that God would help keep His followers united in heart and spirit. Jesus prayed not only for the original disciples, He also petitioned on our behalf. "My prayer is not for them alone. *I pray also for those who will believe in me through their message,* that all of them may be one, Father, just as you are in me and I am in you. May they also be in us so that the world may believe that you have sent me" (John 17:20-21 italics added).

Did you hear that? Jesus was actually praying for you and me! He was asking God to help us walk together through the course of life hand in hand without being divided or disunified. If Jesus prayed for the Father to do it, let's not make any excuses to justify our separation from others. We are to be one, just as God and Jesus are one. We are to Grow Together working hard for complete unity and peace.

Make every effort to keep the unity of the Spirit through the bond of peace. (Ephesians 4:3)

Ready, Set, Grow!

As you close out this final chapter and move forward in your own walk with God, my hope and prayer is that the words of this book have inspired, educated, and empowered you to grow. God has given you everything you need to grow. "His divine power has given us everything we need for a godly life through our knowledge of him who called us by his own glory and goodness" (2 Peter 1:3). So just remember, no matter what you face in this life, the grace of God is able to help you *grow* through it.

You, my friend, were BORN to GROW!

Remember These Truths and Take Action

- You cannot help but grow up if you persistently and consistently read the Bible, pray, and invite the Holy Spirit to take control of your life. You are bound to grow, grow, grow up, and away!
- When it comes to sharing our faith with the world around us, Jesus has given us one big, fat green light. But He first wants us to stop (red light) and wait (yellow light) for His Holy Spirit to empower and enable us.
- The quickest way to grow closer to God is to fix your eyes upon Jesus. Jesus is not only the final stop on the journey; He is also the path along the journey as well.
- In any and every season of life, the journey is always sweeter when the road you travel is not traversed alone because God has called us to Grow Together.

Personal Reflection and Group Discussion Questions

- What is the biggest take-away you have from reading this book?
- What action step do you need to take as a result of reading this book?
- Who do you know that could benefit from a copy of this book?

Meditation

God has room for me to grow.

Prayer

God, help me to grow into the image and likeness of Your Son, Jesus.

Bible References

- 1 Peter 2:2
- Matthew 28:18-20
- Luke 24:49
- John 14:6a
- Hebrews 12:1-3
- Ecclesiastes 4:9-10
- John 17:11
- John 17:20-21
- Ephesians 4:3
- 2 Peter 1:3

Final Word

Imagine, Work, Learn and Grow!

I took my eight year-old son Jordan up on the roof of our single story house the other day to help clean up leaves and branches. Jordan really loves to play and have fun, much more than he likes doing house work, so I often try to make a game out of his chores or find fun ways that he can help out. Getting him up on the roof was a great incentive for him to participate in our fall clean up. The roof is normally forbidden territory for the kids for obvious reasons, but I made this acceptation and gave him some good boundaries of where he had to stand and what was off limits.

"Wow, Dad, it's so cool up here!" Jordan exclaimed as he looked across the neighborhood from his new enlightened vantage point. My plan was working; Jordan was enthralled by his new elevated view.

Our Good, Heavenly Father wants to come alongside us and help us in our spiritual growth. He wants to elevate our ways of thinking to his own and give us a heavenly view of what life can be like when we grow up, out, deeper and together with Him. "Good Father, it's so amazing up here!"

Remember, friend, nothing on this earth or in the heavens above is more amazing than the person of Jesus. When we get a glimpse of Him, we will stand in awe and wonder.

> The Son radiates God's own glory and expresses the very character of God, and he sustains everything by the mighty power

of his command. When he had cleansed us from our sins, he sat down in the place of honor at the right hand of the majestic God in heaven. (Hebrews 1:3, NLT)

Have you heard the song, "I Can Only Imagine" by MercyMe? In this song, the lyrics describe what it would be like to meet Jesus someday in heaven. *Will we stand or kneel? Will we dance or be still? Will we rejoice aloud or be silent? What will it be like to meet Jesus face-to-face? I can only imagine!*

I think imagination may be one of the most underused gifts in our Christian life. **God has given us an imagination for the purpose of helping us see beyond what is today into the future with Him tomorrow.** He wants us to use our imagination in a godly way to give us vision for the future we have in Him. Jordan saw something he was not able to see previously because I changed his view from ground level to roof level. In that moment, his imagination took over. "Dad, what if we could build a zip line to go from one roof to the next?"

I want to encourage you to take a few moments, close your eyes and imagine your life becoming so filled with God's life that you actually live like Jesus. Go ahead, close your eyes and imagine.

Now take a few moments and write down what your life will be like when you become more like Jesus.

- *How will your attitude be different?*
- *How will you speak differently? What will you do differently?*
- *If you really want to grow with God, it starts by putting to use your God given imagination.*

After Jordan was done getting the glimpse of the neighborhood, I put him to work. "Okay now, rake those leaves and put them in this bag." The imagining phase was now over, it was time for work! While I do believe that imagining and dreaming may be underutilized gifts from God, I also realize that if we only imagine and dream, but never act, things won't change. Our vision of a changed life will be nothing more than a pipedream. Jordan and I could have spent the whole afternoon dreaming, goofing off and thinking of all the neat things we could do from the rooftop. "Let's throw water balloons!"

The truth is that we were not up on the roof to throw water balloons, or eggs or any other wet and slimy objects. We were up there for work! God the Father has work for us to do. He wants us to grow up in our salvation and that, my friend, takes a lot of work. "Therefore, my dear friends, as you have always obeyed—not only in my presence, but now much more in my absence—**continue to work out your salvation** with fear and trembling" (Philippians 2:12, emphasis mine)

Growing up, Growing Out, Growing Deeper and Growing Together is going to take work on your part. You are going to have to work on holding your tongue and not saying everything on your mind. You are going to have to work at trusting God regardless of your circumstances. You are going to have to work at inviting people to know God for themselves. You are going to have to work at developing a meaningful relationship with God. You are going to have to work at building deep and open friendships with others. Friend, this Christian growth thing is going to take some real work!

As Jordan and I were working he pointed out a tree to me. "Look Dad, that's *the tree*!" The tree he was pointing to was an Oak that had sprouted the same year Jordan was born. "Dad," he continued, "that tree is just as old as me"! We stood there together necks flexed all the way back looking up and admiring this tree that now towers over our house.

Jokingly I said to my son, "Jordan, that tree cannot be the same age as you. Look how tall it is!"

Jordan explained, "Dad, it's a tree. Trees grow faster than people".

"That's no excuse, Jordan. You really need to grow taller! You need to catch up with that tree!" Jordan knew I was joking and we both laughed together as we stood side-by-side on the shingles.

It would be a mistake for any eight year-old to compare himself to an Oak tree his own age. The scales are always going to be tipped in the tree's favor. Take it from Jordan, "Trees grow faster than people." Too often we make the mistake of comparing our lives and progress to that of others. If someone has reached the heavens in their walk with God and you still feel like you're on planet earth – rejoice and be glad! Your

Father in heaven is not comparing your growth to any other children of His.

The Apostle Paul put it this way, "We do not dare to classify or compare ourselves with some who commend themselves. When they measure themselves by themselves and compare themselves with themselves, they are not wise" (2 Corinthians 10:12). Did you catch that? **It is not wise to compare yourself with others, plain and simple.**

While comparing ourselves to others is not wise, **it is wise to learn from others who are growing steadily in their faith.** So if you see some other trees, I mean people, around you who seem to be growing off the charts, don't get discouraged or envious; just take their lives as an object lesson and ask yourself, or them directly if you have the opportunity, "What is making you grow?" What are the habits, actions and attitudes that are being fostered in this person's life that are amounting to such spiritual growth?

Learning from nature is not a bad idea either. Take the Oak tree for example. Little by little that tree grew from a tiny seedling into a strong, healthy, leaf bearing tree. The Oak tree teaches us the power of consistent, but perpetual growth. The same holds true for you and me. Jesus put it this way, "I am the vine; you are the branches. If you remain in me and I in you, you will bear much fruit; apart from me you can do nothing" (John 15:5).

The promise of Jesus is that if we stick with it, or better yet with Him, we will continue to grow and bear fruit. Like a tree branch connected to the trunk, we only find life when we are connected to God in a vibrant, loving relationship. Apart from Him, we are nothing to speak of, but with Him we can grow perpetually bearing ever-increasing fruit.

- *Imagine and dream of yourself becoming like Jesus.*
- *Take action, working with God on your heart, habits, attitudes and behavior.*
- *Don't compare yourself with others, but learn from those who are growing.*

My prayer for you is this:

May the Lord bless, empower, strengthen and equip you with the love and grace needed to grow up, to grow out, to grow deeper and grow together. May you always know and have confidence in the truth that God is working everything for your ultimate good, to be like Jesus. May you one day meet Jesus face-to-face and it be as if you were seeing a reflection of yourself. Let it be so!

"But grow in the grace and knowledge of our
Lord and Savior Jesus Christ.

To him be glory both now and forever! Amen."

(2 Peter 3:18)

About the Author

Pierre M. Eade is a teacher, pastor, inspirational speaker, evangelist and life coach. His life vision is to inspire, educate, lead and empower people to grow up, grow out, grow deeper and grow together. He graduated with distinctions from Liberty University with a master's degree in Evangelism and Church Planting. His writings on the Christian life and spiritual growth can be found on his internationally visited website: www.christiangrowthnetwork.com. On his website, you can also join his mailing list, contact Pierre for speaking engagements, or personal life coaching and purchase additional copies of this book.

Made in the USA
Lexington, KY
18 March 2018